Mini Crock Pot
COOKBOOK
For Beginners
2025

LUIS F. HILL

CONTENT

GRATITUDE

Dear Reader,

Congratulations on picking up your copy of this book! I'm so excited to join you on your culinary adventure, helping you create easy, mouthwatering meals with your mini crock pot. Whether you're brand new to slow cooking or a seasoned pro looking for new ideas, this book has been designed with you in mind—making home-cooked meals more accessible, fun, and flavorful.

Thank you for allowing me to be part of your kitchen! I've filled these pages with my favorite tried-and-true recipes, and I'm confident you'll find plenty of inspiration as you explore.

As a token of my gratitude, I've included a special bonus just for you! Don't forget to check out page 113 for something extra that will add even more variety and convenience to your cooking.

Happy cooking, and here's to many delicious moments ahead!

With gratitude,

Dr. Luis

Introduction

introduce you to the world of slow cooking in a way that's approachable and enjoyable.

The mini crock pot is your new kitchen companion, perfect for small households, single servings, or even a cozy dinner for two. With this versatile tool, you can whip up a variety of dishes, from hearty breakfasts to comforting dinners, without spending hours in the kitchen. Instead of standing over a stove, you can simply prepare your ingredients, set your mini crock pot, and let it work its magic while you focus on your day.

This cookbook is crafted with beginners in mind, ensuring that each recipe is not only delicious but also easy to follow. We'll walk you through everything you need to know to get started, so even if you've never used a crock pot before, by the time you finish this book, you'll feel like a pro.

Why a Mini Crock Pot?

You might be wondering, why choose a mini crock pot over other kitchen appliances? The answer lies in its unique combination of convenience, efficiency, and versatility.

Welcome to a culinary journey that combines simplicity, convenience, and flavor—all packed into a compact, easy-to-use appliance: the mini crock pot. Whether you're a busy professional, a student, or someone who simply enjoys the art of slow cooking, this cookbook is designed to

- <u>**Perfect for Small Portions:**</u> Unlike standard-sized crock pots, the mini version is ideal for cooking smaller portions, which means less waste and perfectly sized meals. It's great for singles, couples, or even those looking to prepare a quick side dish without using a larger appliance.

- **Space-Saving Design:** If you have a small kitchen or limited storage, a mini crock pot is the perfect solution. It takes up minimal counter space and can easily be tucked away when not in use, making it ideal for apartments, dorms, or RVs.

- **Energy Efficient:** Because of its size, a mini crock pot uses less energy compared to larger slow cookers or ovens, making it an eco-friendly option that won't spike your electricity bill.

- **Ease of Use:** The simplicity of the mini crock pot is one of its most appealing features. With just a few settings—typically low, high, and warm—it's easy to operate even for those who are new to cooking. Simply set it and forget it, letting the slow cooking process bring out the rich, developed flavors in your food.

- **Versatility:** Don't let its size fool you; a mini crock pot is incredibly versatile. You can prepare a wide range of dishes, from soups and stews to desserts and dips, all with minimal effort. It's an excellent tool for experimenting with different cuisines and flavors.

Tips for Slow Cooking Success

To make the most of your mini crock pot, it's important to understand a few basic principles of slow cooking. These tips will help you achieve delicious results every time.

1. **Layering is Key:** When adding ingredients to your crock pot, consider the order in which you layer them. Denser, heavier ingredients like root vegetables (carrots, potatoes) should go on the bottom, closest to the heat source. This ensures they cook evenly and are perfectly tender by the time your dish is ready.

2. **Don't Overfill:** Your mini crock pot works best when it's filled between half and three-quarters full. Overfilling can lead to uneven cooking, while underfilling might cause your food to dry out. Stick to recipes designed for your mini crock pot's capacity for the best results.

3. **Keep the Lid On:** Resist the temptation to lift the lid and check on your food. Each time you remove the lid, heat escapes, extending the cooking time and potentially affecting the final outcome. Trust the process, and only lift the lid when it's necessary to stir or add ingredients.

4. **Prep Ingredients for Even Cooking:** For the best texture and flavor, chop your ingredients into uniform pieces. This ensures that everything cooks at

the same rate, avoiding undercooked or overcooked spots.

5. <u>Use the Right Cut of Meat:</u> Slow cooking is perfect for tenderizing tougher cuts of meat. Opt for cuts like chuck roast, pork shoulder, or chicken thighs, which benefit from the low and slow cooking method, resulting in tender, flavorful dishes.

6. <u>Adjust Seasonings Wisely:</u> Flavors tend to concentrate during the slow cooking process. Start with a light hand on seasonings, especially salt, and adjust to taste toward the end of cooking. This helps prevent overly salty or spiced dishes.

7. <u>Add Dairy Later:</u> If your recipe includes dairy products like milk, cream, or cheese, add them during the last 30 minutes of cooking to prevent curdling.

Essential Tools and Ingredients for Beginners

Before you dive into the recipes, it's important to have a few basic tools and ingredients on hand. These will make your cooking experience smoother and more enjoyable.

Tools:

1. <u>Mini Crock Pot:</u> The star of the show! Ensure you have a reliable mini crock pot that suits your needs. Most recipes in this book are designed for a 1.5 to 2.5-quart crock pot.

2. <u>Measuring Cups and Spoons:</u> Accurate measurements are key to achieving consistent results, especially when following a recipe.

3. <u>Sharp Knife and Cutting Board:</u> Essential for prepping ingredients, a sharp knife will make chopping vegetables and meats easier and safer.

4. Mixing Bowls: Useful for prepping and combining ingredients before they go into the crock pot.

5. Wooden Spoons and Spatulas: These are gentle on your crock pot's surface and perfect for stirring and serving.

6. Food Storage Containers: Ideal for storing leftovers or prepping ingredients in advance.

Ingredients:

1. <u>Aromatic Vegetables:</u> Onions, garlic, celery, and carrots are the building blocks of flavor in many slow-cooked dishes.

2. <u>Broths and Stocks:</u> Keep a variety of broths (chicken, beef, vegetable) on hand to add depth to soups, stews, and braised dishes.

3. <u>Spices and Herbs:</u> A well-stocked spice cabinet is essential. Start with basics like salt, pepper, paprika, cumin, thyme, and bay leaves.

4. <u>Canned Goods:</u> Items like diced tomatoes, beans, and coconut milk are pantry staples that add richness and flavor to many recipes.

5. <u>Grains and Legumes:</u> Rice, quinoa, lentils, and beans are great additions to slow-cooked meals, providing texture and substance.

6. <u>Protein Sources:</u> Whether you prefer meat, poultry, seafood, or plant-based proteins, having a variety on hand allows for flexibility in meal planning.

7. <u>Dairy and Non-Dairy Alternatives:</u> Depending on your dietary preferences, keep some milk, cream, cheese, or plant-based alternatives ready for adding creaminess to your dishes.

How to Make the Most of This Cookbook

This cookbook is more than just a collection of recipes—it's a guide to becoming confident in the kitchen with your mini crock pot. Here's exactly how to get the most out of it:

- **Start Simple:** Begin with the easier recipes to familiarize yourself with your mini crock pot and the slow cooking process. Then as you gain confidence, move on to more complex dishes.

- **Experiment and Customize:** Feel free to tweak the recipes to suit your taste. Add extra herbs, switch up the proteins, or try a new vegetable. The mini crock pot is very forgiving, so don't be afraid to get creative.

- **Meal Prep and Plan:** Use your mini crock pot to batch cook meals for the week. Many of the recipes in this book can be easily doubled or even tripled and then portioned out for future meals, this is especially handy for those with busy schedules.

- **Utilize the "Keep Warm" Setting:** If your mini crock pot has a "keep warm" setting, use it to maintain the temperature of your dish until you're ready to serve. This is perfect for entertaining or when your meal finishes cooking before you're ready to eat.

- **Master the Basics, Then Expand:** Once you're comfortable with the foundational recipes, try branching out into the global flavors and more intricate dishes included in later chapters. This will help you expand your culinary horizons and deepen your slow-cooking skills.

- **Savor the Experience:** Slow cooking is not just about the food; it's about the process. Enjoy the aroma that fills your home as your meal slowly cooks, and take pride in the delicious, wholesome food you've created.

By following these guidelines and using this cookbook as your companion, you'll quickly discover how easy and enjoyable mini crock pot cooking can be. Whether you're preparing a simple meal for yourself or hosting a small dinner party, your mini crock pot will become an indispensable tool in your kitchen arsenal. Here's to delicious, stress-free cooking!

Chapter 1.

Breakfast Bliss

Introduction to Breakfast Bliss

Breakfast is often called the most important meal of the day, and of course with good reason. It sets the tone for your energy levels, mood, and focus as you start your day. In this chapter, "Breakfast Bliss," we'll explore a variety of mini crock pot recipes that make it easy to enjoy a nourishing, flavorful breakfast, even on the busiest mornings.

From comforting bowls of oatmeal simmering with sweet spices to protein-packed casseroles bursting with fresh veggies, these recipes are designed to be both delicious and convenient. With your mini crock pot, you can prepare breakfast the night before, waking up to a warm, ready-to-eat meal that fuels your day from the first bite. Whether you're feeding a family or just yourself, these breakfasts will make your mornings a little more blissful.

Cinnamon Apple Oatmeal

set up the night before and wake up to a hearty, ready-to-eat meal that fuels your day with wholesome goodness.

Preparation Time

- **Prep Time:** 10 minutes
- **Cooking Time:** 6–8 hours (overnight)
- **Total Time:** 6 hours and 10 minutes to 8 hours and 10 minutes

Ingredients:

- Steel-cut oats: 1 cup
- Apples (peeled, cored, and diced): 2 medium-sized (Granny Smith or Honeycrisp recommended)
- Cinnamon: 1 ½ teaspoons
- Nutmeg: ¼ teaspoon
- Pure vanilla extract: 1 teaspoon
- Maple syrup or honey: 2 tablespoons (adjust to taste)
- Water: 3 cups
- Unsweetened almond milk (or any milk of choice): 1 cup
- Pinch of salt: Optional, to enhance flavor
- Chopped nuts (walnuts or pecans) or dried fruits (raisins, cranberries) for garnish: Optional

Serving Size

Serves: 4

Procedure

1. **Prep the Ingredients:** Start by peeling, coring, and dicing the apples into small, even pieces. This helps them

Start your day with a warm, comforting bowl of Cinnamon Apple Oatmeal, a breakfast that's not only delicious but also incredibly nourishing. This recipe harnesses the natural sweetness of apples combined with the warm spice of cinnamon, slow-cooked to creamy perfection in your mini crock pot. It's a fuss-free breakfast that you can cook evenly and blend well with the oats.

2. **Combine Ingredients in the Crock Pot:** In your mini crock pot (1.5 to 2.5 quarts), add the steel-cut oats, diced apples, cinnamon, nutmeg, vanilla extract, and a pinch of salt if using. Pour in the water and almond milk, and give everything a good stir to combine.

3. **Sweeten It:** Drizzle the maple syrup or honey over the mixture. You can adjust the sweetness later, but starting with a small amount helps balance the flavors as they develop.

4. **Cook:** Cover the mini crock pot with its lid and set it to low. Cook for 6–8 hours. This is perfect for preparing before bed, as the slow cooker will work overnight, allowing the oats to absorb the flavors and achieve a creamy texture.

5. **Check and Serve:** In the morning, give the oatmeal a good stir. If it's thicker than you like, you can add a splash of almond milk or water to reach your desired consistency. Taste and add more maple syrup or honey if needed. Serve warm, topped with chopped nuts or dried fruits for added texture and flavor.

6. **Store and Reheat:** Leftovers can be stored in an airtight container in the refrigerator for up to 3 days. Reheat individual portions in the microwave with a splash of milk to loosen the oatmeal.

Nutritional Value (Per Serving)

- **Calories:** Approximately 210 kcal
- **Protein:** 5g
- **Fat:** 4g (with almonds or nuts as garnish)
- **Carbohydrates:** 40g
- **Fiber:** 6g
- **Sugars:** 12g (including natural sugars from apples and maple syrup)
- **Vitamin C:** 5mg
- **Calcium:** 130mg
- **Iron:** 2mg

Cooking Tips

- **Use Steel-Cut Oats:** Steel-cut oats are ideal for slow cooking because they hold their shape and texture much better than rolled oats, which can become mushy. If you only have rolled oats on hand, reduce the cooking time to 3–4 hours on low.

- **Prevent Sticking:** If you notice that your oatmeal tends to stick to the sides of the crock pot, you can lightly grease the interior with a small amount of coconut oil or maybe cooking spray before adding the ingredients.

- **Adjust Consistency:** If your oatmeal is too thick after cooking, stir in additional almond milk or water until it reaches your preferred consistency. If it's too thin, remove the lid and let it cook for an additional 15-30 minutes on high to evaporate some of the liquid.

- **Add Texture:** For a bit of crunch, stir in some chopped nuts right before serving. Alternatively, a handful of dried fruits like raisins or cranberries adds a delightful chewiness and a burst of sweetness.

- **Enhance Flavors:** If you're a fan of spice, consider adding a pinch of cloves or allspice to the mix for a deeper flavor profile.

Health Benefits

- **Rich in Fiber:** Steel-cut oats are an excellent source of dietary fiber, particularly soluble fiber, which helps stabilize blood sugar levels, supports heart health, and promotes digestive health.

- **Antioxidant-Rich:** Apples are packed with antioxidants, especially when you include the skin. These compounds help fight inflammation and reduce the risk of chronic diseases.

- **Heart-Healthy:** Cinnamon has been shown to help lower blood sugar levels and improve heart health by reducing cholesterol and triglycerides.

- **Sustained Energy:** The complex carbohydrates in oats provide a slow and steady release of energy, keeping you full and satisfied throughout the morning.

- **Low in Added Sugars:** By sweetening your oatmeal naturally with apples and just a touch of maple syrup or honey, you're enjoying a breakfast that's low in added sugars, which is beneficial for maintaining stable blood sugar levels.

- **Bone Health:** Almond milk is a good source of calcium and vitamin D, essential for maintaining strong bones and preventing osteoporosis.

Cinnamon Apple Oatmeal is more than just a breakfast—it's a nourishing, comforting start to your day that's incredibly easy to prepare. By using your mini crock pot, you can enjoy a warm, hearty meal that's ready when you wake up, making your mornings less rushed and more enjoyable. With its blend of whole grains, fruits, and spices, this oatmeal offers a balance of nutrients that support overall health while satisfying your taste buds. Whether you're new to slow cooking or a seasoned pro, this recipe is sure to become a staple in your breakfast routine.

Veggie-Packed Breakfast Casserole

when you need a wholesome meal that's ready to go. This recipe is designed to be cooked overnight in your mini crock pot, allowing you to wake up to a warm, hearty breakfast that will fuel you for hours.

Preparation Time

- **Prep Time:** 20 minutes
- **Cooking Time:** 7–8 hours (overnight) or 4–5 hours on high
- **Total Time:** 7 hours and 20 minutes to 8 hours and 20 minutes

Ingredients

- Eggs: 8 large
- Milk (whole or your preferred type): 1 cup
- Red bell pepper (diced): 1 medium
- Green bell pepper (diced): 1 medium
- Onion (diced): 1 small
- Spinach (fresh, roughly chopped): 2 cups
- Mushrooms (sliced): 1 cup
- Cheddar cheese (shredded): 1 cup
- Parmesan cheese (grated): ¼ cup
- Garlic (minced): 2 cloves
- Salt: 1 teaspoon
- Black pepper: ½ teaspoon
- Olive oil: 1 tablespoon
- Optional: Fresh herbs (maybe parsley or chives), chopped, for garnish

Serving Size

Serves: 4–6

Procedure

1. **Prep the Vegetables:** Start by washing and preparing your vegetables. Dice the bell peppers, onion, and slice the

The Veggie-Packed Breakfast Casserole is a nutritious and satisfying way to kickstart your day. Bursting with vibrant vegetables, eggs, and cheese, this dish offers a balanced blend of protein, fiber, and essential vitamins. It's perfect for those busy mornings

mushrooms. Roughly chop the spinach.

2. **Sauté the Vegetables: Heat** the olive oil in a medium-sized skillet over medium heat. Add the diced onion, bell peppers, and mushrooms. Sauté for 5-7 minutes until the vegetables are soft and the onions are translucent. Add the minced garlic and simmer for another minute, or until fragrant. Finally, stir in the spinach and cook until it just wilts, about 1-2 minutes. Remove from heat.

3. **Make the Egg Mixture:** In a large mixing bowl, whisk together the eggs, milk, salt, and pepper until thoroughly blended.

4. **Layer the Ingredients in the Mini Crock Pot:** Lightly grease the inside of your mini crock pot (1.5 to 2.5 quarts) with a bit of olive oil or cooking spray. Begin by spreading half of the sautéed vegetable mixture at the bottom. Sprinkle half of the shredded cheddar cheese over the veggies. Pour half of the egg mixture over the cheese and vegetables. Repeat the layers with the remaining vegetables, cheese, and egg mixture. Finally, go ahead and sprinkle the grated Parmesan cheese on top.

5. **Cook:** Cover the mini crock pot with its lid and cook on low for 7-8 hours or on high for 4-5 hours, until the eggs are

set and the casserole is firm in the center.

6. **Serve:** Once cooked, allow the casserole to cool slightly before slicing. Garnish with fresh herbs if desired. Serve warm.

7. **Store and Reheat:** Leftovers can be stored in an airtight container in the refrigerator for up to 3 days. To reheat, warm individual portions in the microwave or oven until heated through.

Nutritional Value (Per Serving, Based on 6 Servings)

- **Calories:** Approximately 200 kcal
- **Protein:** 13g
- **Fat:** 14g
- **Carbohydrates:** 7g
- **Fiber:** 2g
- **Sugars:** 3g
- **Vitamin A:** 1800 IU
- **Vitamin C:** 40mg
- **Calcium:** 200mg
- **Iron:** 2mg

Cooking Tips

- **Customize Your Veggies:** Feel free to mix and match your vegetables based on what you have on hand. Zucchini, tomatoes, or even kale can be great additions to this casserole. Just be mindful of water content in some veggies; sautéing them first helps remove excess moisture.

- **Prevent Overcooking:** If cooking overnight, make sure to check the casserole early in the morning. Depending on your crock pot's heat settings, it might be done closer to the 7-hour mark. You don't want the eggs to overcook and become rubbery.

- **Cheese Variations:** While cheddar and Parmesan provide a classic flavor, you can experiment with other cheeses like feta, mozzarella, or Gruyère for different taste profiles.

- **Meat Additions:** If you'd like to add meat to your casserole, cooked and crumbled sausage, bacon, or diced ham work wonderfully. Just make sure they're fully cooked before adding to the crock pot.

- **Grease the Crock Pot Well:** To prevent the casserole from sticking, be generous with the olive oil or cooking spray. This also makes cleanup much easier.

- **For a Lighter Version:** You can use egg whites or a combination of whole eggs and egg whites to reduce the fat content. Low-fat cheese and skim milk can also be used.

Health Benefits

- **High in Protein:** Eggs are a fantastic source of high-quality protein, which is essential for muscle repair, growth, and overall body maintenance. A protein-rich breakfast can also help keep you full and satisfied until your next meal.

- **Rich in Vitamins and Minerals:** This casserole is packed with vegetables that provide essential vitamins and minerals. Bell peppers are loaded with vitamin C, while spinach offers a good dose of iron and folate. Mushrooms add a boost of B vitamins and minerals like selenium.

- **Supports Heart Health:** The combination of eggs and vegetables offers a balanced meal rich in heart-healthy nutrients. Eggs contain healthy fats and antioxidants like lutein and zeaxanthin, which are beneficial for heart and eye health.

- **Boosts Immunity:** The vitamin C in bell peppers and the garlic in this recipe contribute to a stronger immune system, helping to ward off colds and other illnesses.

- **Maintains Healthy Weight:** Starting your day with a protein and fiber-rich meal can help control appetite and reduce the likelihood of overeating later in the day. The fiber from the vegetables aids in digestion and helps maintain a healthy weight.

- <u>Low in Carbohydrates:</u> This casserole is relatively low in carbs, making it suitable for those following a low-carb or keto diet. The vegetables provide essential nutrients without adding unnecessary carbs or sugars.

The Veggie-Packed Breakfast Casserole is an excellent choice for anyone looking to enjoy a nutritious, flavorful start to their day. It's an easy, make-ahead dish that can be customized to your liking, making it versatile enough for any taste or dietary preference. With its blend of protein, fiber, and essential vitamins, this casserole is not only filling but also provides a balanced meal that supports overall health and well-being. Whether you're feeding your family or prepping meals for the week, this recipe is sure to become a favorite in your breakfast rotation.

Overnight Vanilla Almond Quinoa

Overnight Vanilla Almond Quinoa is a delicious and nutritious breakfast that's perfect for busy mornings. This recipe takes the wholesome goodness of quinoa and transforms it into a creamy, satisfying dish infused with the sweet flavor of vanilla and the nutty richness of almonds. By preparing it in your mini crock pot overnight, you can wake up to a warm, ready-to-eat meal that's high in protein, packed with fiber, and naturally gluten-free. It's an excellent alternative to traditional oatmeal, offering a unique texture and a delightful taste.

Preparation Time

- **Prep Time:** 10 minutes
- **Cooking Time:** 6–8 hours (overnight)
- **Total Time:** 6 hours and 10 minutes to 8 hours and 10 minutes

Ingredients

- Quinoa: 1 cup (rinsed well under cold water)
- Almond milk (unsweetened or your preferred milk): 2 cups
- Water: 1 cup
- Pure vanilla extract: 1 ½ teaspoons
- Maple syrup or honey: 2 tablespoons (adjust to taste)
- Almonds (sliced or slivered): ¼ cup (plus extra for topping)
- Ground cinnamon: ½ teaspoon
- Pinch of salt: Optional
- Fresh or dried fruit (such as berries, sliced banana, or raisins) for topping: Optional
- Chia seeds or flax seeds: Optional, for added nutrition

Serving Size

Serves: 4

Procedure

1. **Prepare the Quinoa:** Start by thoroughly rinsing the quinoa under cold water in a fine-mesh sieve. This step is crucial to remove the natural coating called saponin, which can give quinoa a bitter taste.

2. **Combine Ingredients in the Crock Pot:** In your mini crock pot (1.5 to 2.5 quarts), add the rinsed quinoa, almond milk, water, vanilla extract, maple syrup or honey, sliced almonds, ground cinnamon, and also a pinch of salt if using. Stir to combine all the ingredients properly.

3. **Cook:** Cover the mini crock pot with its lid and set it to low. Allow the quinoa to cook for 6–8 hours. The slow cooking process will allow the quinoa to absorb the liquid, resulting in a creamy and flavorful breakfast.

4. **Check and Serve:** In the morning, give the quinoa a good stir. If it appears too thick, add a splash of almond milk or water to achieve your desired consistency. Taste and adjust the sweetness if needed by adding a bit more maple syrup or honey. Serve warm, topped with additional sliced almonds, fresh or dried fruit, and a sprinkle of chia seeds or flax seeds if desired.

5. **Store and Reheat:** Leftovers can be stored in an airtight container in the refrigerator for up to 3 days. Reheat individual portions in the microwave, adding a splash of almond milk or water to loosen the consistency.

Nutritional Value (Per Serving)

- **Calories:** Approximately 220 kcal
- **Protein:** 7g
- **Fat:** 7g
- **Carbohydrates:** 33g
- **Fiber:** 5g
- **Sugars:** 7g (from maple syrup or honey)
- **Calcium:** 120mg
- **Iron:** 2.5mg
- **Magnesium:** 80mg

Cooking Tips

- **Rinse the Quinoa Thoroughly:** Always rinse quinoa under cold water before cooking to remove the saponin, which can cause a bitter taste. This step ensures a more pleasant flavor in the final dish.

- **Adjust Sweetness to Taste:** Depending on your preference, you can adjust the sweetness by adding more or less maple syrup or honey. You can also use a sugar-free sweetener if you prefer.

- **Mix Up the Toppings:** Feel free to customize the toppings to suit your taste. Fresh berries, banana slices, dried fruits like raisins or cranberries, and nuts such as walnuts or pecans all make excellent additions. For added nutrition, consider topping with chia seeds, flax seeds, or even a dollop of almond butter.

- **Control the Consistency:** If the quinoa seems too thick in the morning, simply stir in a bit more almond milk or water until it reaches your desired consistency. Conversely, if it's too thin, let it sit uncovered in the crock pot on the warm setting for 15–30 minutes to thicken up.

- **Use Other Milk Alternatives:** While almond milk adds a subtle nutty flavor, you can substitute it with any other milk you prefer, such as coconut milk, soy milk, or oat milk, depending on your specific dietary needs and taste preferences.

- **Add Protein:** For an extra protein boost, you can stir in a scoop of vanilla protein powder after cooking, or mix in a spoonful of Greek yogurt when serving.

Health Benefits

- **High Protein Content:** Quinoa is of course a complete protein, which means it includes all the nine essential amino acids that the body cannot manufacture on its own. This is exactly what makes it an ideal protein source, particularly for vegetarians and vegans.

- **Rich in Fiber:** This dish is high in dietary fiber, which is beneficial for digestive health, helping to prevent constipation and maintain a healthy gut. Fiber also helps regulate blood sugar levels and can contribute to heart health by lowering cholesterol.

- **Gluten-Free:** Quinoa is naturally gluten-free, making this recipe a safe and nutritious option for those with celiac disease or gluten sensitivity.

- **Packed with Essential Nutrients:** Quinoa is a good source of several important vitamins and minerals, including magnesium, iron, and B vitamins. These nutrients support everything from energy production to bone health and immune function.

- **Low Glycemic Index:** Quinoa has a low glycemic index, meaning it provides a slow and steady release of energy, which can help keep blood sugar levels stable and prevent energy crashes.

- **Antioxidant-Rich:** The addition of almonds provides healthy fats, vitamin E, and antioxidants, which help fight inflammation and protect your cells from oxidative stress.

- **Supports Weight Management:** The combination of protein, fiber, and healthy fats in this dish promotes satiety, helping you feel full for longer and reducing the likelihood of overeating later in the day.

- **Bone Health:** Almond milk, especially if fortified, can be a good source of calcium and vitamin D, both of which are essential for maintaining strong bones and preventing osteoporosis.

- **Boosts Heart Health:** The unsaturated fats found in almonds, along with the fiber from quinoa, contribute to heart health by lowering LDL (bad) cholesterol levels and reducing the risk of heart disease.

Overnight Vanilla Almond Quinoa is a nourishing, flavorful breakfast that's perfect for starting your day on a healthy note. It's a fantastic alternative to traditional oatmeal, offering a rich, creamy texture with the added benefits of high-quality plant-based protein and fiber. This easy-to-prepare dish is ideal for those with busy mornings, allowing you to enjoy a warm, satisfying meal without the morning rush. With its versatility and health benefits, this recipe is sure to become a favorite in your breakfast rotation.

Slow-Cooker Banana Nut Quinoa Porridge

sweetness and satisfying crunch. It's ideal for anyone looking for a nutrient-dense breakfast that keeps you full and energized for hours.

Preparation Time

- **Prep Time:** 5 minutes
- **Cook Time:** 2-3 hours on low

Serving Size

Servings: 2

Ingredients:

- ½ cup quinoa, rinsed well
- One (1) cup unsweetened almond milk (or any milk of choice)
- 1 cup water
- 1 medium ripe banana, mashed
- 1 tablespoon pure maple syrup or honey (optional for sweetness)
- 1 teaspoon vanilla extract
- ½ teaspoon ground cinnamon
- ¼ teaspoon ground nutmeg
- Pinch of salt
- 2 tablespoons chopped walnuts or pecans (for topping)
- Extra banana slices for serving (optional)

Procedure:

1. **Prepare the Crock Pot:** Lightly grease the inside of your mini crock pot with non-stick spray or a small amount of oil to prevent sticking.

2. Rinse the Quinoa: Thoroughly rinse the quinoa under cold water using a fine mesh strainer to remove its natural bitter coating (saponins).

This Slow-Cooker Banana Nut Quinoa Porridge is a hearty, protein-packed breakfast that's perfect for busy mornings. Quinoa offers a gluten-free, high-protein alternative to traditional grains, while the bananas and nuts provide a natural

3. Combine Ingredients: In the mini crock pot, add the rinsed quinoa, almond milk, water, mashed banana, vanilla extract, cinnamon, nutmeg, and a pinch of salt. Stir the mixture to combine all ingredients evenly.

4. Cook: Cover the crock pot with the lid and cook on low for 2-3 hours, or until the quinoa is soft and fully cooked. Stir the porridge halfway through cooking to ensure it cooks evenly and doesn't stick to the sides.

5. Final Touch: Once the quinoa is tender, give the porridge a final stir. If it's too thick, add a splash of almond milk or water to reach your desired consistency.

6. Serve: Scoop the porridge into bowls and top with chopped walnuts or pecans, along with extra banana slices for added sweetness. Now you drizzle with maple syrup or honey if desired.

Nutritional Value (Per Serving):

- **Calories:** ~320
- **Protein:** ~9g
- **Fat:** ~10g (mostly from healthy fats in the nuts)
- **Carbohydrates:** ~47g
- **Fiber:** ~6g
- **Sugar:** ~12g (from banana and optional maple syrup)

- **Vitamins & Minerals:** High in potassium, magnesium, and vitamin B6 from the banana, plus iron and calcium from quinoa.

Cooking Tips:

- **Quinoa Rinsing:** Make sure to rinse quinoa thoroughly to remove its natural bitter taste. This is an essential step to enhance the flavor of your porridge.
- **Banana Ripeness:** For the best sweetness and texture, use a ripe banana. The natural sugars in ripe bananas will sweeten the porridge without needing extra sweeteners.
- **Customization:** You can swap the walnuts for other nuts like pecans or almonds, or add seeds like chia or flax for additional nutrients.
- **Texture Adjustment:** If you prefer a creamier porridge, add an extra ¼ cup of almond milk at the end of cooking and stir it in.
- **Advanced Prep:** You can prepare the ingredients the night before and simply set the crock pot on low in the morning, so your porridge is ready to eat by the time you're up.

Health Benefits:

- **High in Protein:** Quinoa of course is a complete protein, meaning that it contains all nine essential amino acids. This makes it a fantastic plant-based protein option for vegetarians and vegans.

- **Rich in Fiber:** Quinoa and bananas are excellent sources of dietary fiber, which supports healthy digestion and keeps you feeling full longer. Fiber also helps regulate blood sugar and cholesterol levels of the body.

- **Heart-Healthy Fats:** The walnuts or pecans provide a good dose of heart-healthy omega-3 fatty acids, which are beneficial for cardiovascular health and reducing inflammation.

- **Energy Boosting:** Bananas are a natural source of carbohydrates and potassium, which are great for maintaining energy levels and supporting muscle function, especially in the morning.

- **Gluten-Free:** Quinoa is naturally gluten-free, making this porridge an excellent option for individuals with gluten sensitivities or celiac disease.

- **Low-Glycemic:** Quinoa has a low glycemic index, meaning it releases energy slowly, which helps avoid blood sugar spikes and keeps you feeling satisfied longer.

This recipe offers an ideal balance of healthy fats, protein, and fiber to ensure you start the day on the right foot, with long-lasting energy and plenty of nutrients!

Mini Crock Pot Southwest Egg Scramble

It's perfect for those who want a savory, filling breakfast with minimal effort. This low-carb meal is packed with essential nutrients and can be customized to suit different tastes and dietary needs.

Preparation Time

- **Prep Time:** 10 minutes
- **Cook Time:** 2-3 hours on low

Serving Size

Servings: 2

Ingredients:

- 4 large eggs
- ¼ cup unsweetened almond milk (or any milk of choice)
- ¼ cup diced bell peppers
- ¼ cup diced onion
- ¼ cup black beans (rinsed and drained)
- ¼ cup shredded cheddar cheese (optional)
- 1 small jalapeño, diced (optional)
- 2 tablespoons salsa (plus more for serving)
- ¼ teaspoon cumin
- ¼ teaspoon smoked paprika
- ¼ teaspoon garlic powder
- Salt and pepper to taste
- 1 tablespoon chopped fresh cilantro (optional)
- Non-stick spray or oil for greasing

Procedure:

1. **Grease the Crock Pot:** Lightly grease the mini crock pot with non-stick spray or a small amount of oil.

The Mini Crock Pot Southwest Egg Scramble is a flavorful, protein-rich breakfast that combines eggs, black beans, veggies, and bold Southwestern spices.

2. <u>Prep the Veggies:</u> Dice the bell peppers, onion, and jalapeño (if using).

3. <u>Whisk the Eggs:</u> In a bowl, whisk together eggs, almond milk, cumin, paprika, garlic powder, salt, and pepper. Stir in the veggies, black beans, and salsa.

4. <u>Cook:</u> Pour the mixture into the crock pot. Add cheese on top if desired. Cover and cook on low for 2-3 hours, or until the eggs are fully set.

5. <u>Serve:</u> Garnish with fresh cilantro and serve with sliced avocado, extra salsa, or a dollop of sour cream.

Nutritional Value (Per Serving):

- <u>Calories:</u> ~230 (without cheese); ~300 (with cheese)
- <u>Protein:</u> ~18g
- <u>Fat:</u> ~14g
- <u>Carbs:</u> ~10g
- <u>Fiber:</u> ~4g
- <u>Vitamins & Minerals:</u> Rich in vitamins A, C, and B, plus iron and potassium from the eggs and vegetables.

Cooking Tips:

- <u>Control the Heat:</u> Use mild salsa and omit the jalapeño for a gentler flavor, or add extra jalapeño and hot salsa for more spice.

- <u>Dairy-Free Option:</u> Omit the cheese or use a plant-based alternative.

- <u>Meal Prep:</u> Make this ahead of time and store it in the fridge for up to 3 days. Reheat when needed.

- <u>Add More Veggies:</u> Feel free to add spinach, mushrooms, or zucchini to the scramble for extra nutrients.

Health Benefits:

- <u>Protein-Packed:</u> Eggs provide high-quality protein, which is essential for muscle repair and overall body function. Black beans add a plant-based protein boost, making this a satisfying breakfast option.

- <u>Low-Carb & Fiber-Rich:</u> With only 10g of carbohydrates, this scramble fits well in low-carb or ketogenic diets. The fiber from black beans helps maintain steady blood sugar levels and supports digestive health.

- <u>Heart-Healthy Fats:</u> Avocado and eggs are rich in healthy fats, especially monounsaturated fats and omega-3s, which promote heart health and reduce inflammation.

- <u>Antioxidant Powerhouse:</u> Bell peppers, onions, and salsa are rich in vitamins A and C, providing antioxidants that support immune health, reduce inflammation, and promote healthy skin.

- **<u>Customizable and Nutrient-Dense:</u>** This dish is packed with vitamins and minerals like iron, potassium, and vitamin B6, which are important for energy, brain function, and immune support.

The Mini Crock Pot Southwest Egg Scramble is a nutrient-dense, versatile breakfast that's easy to prepare and bursting with flavor. With a great balance of protein, healthy fats, and fiber, this low-carb dish keeps you full and energized throughout the morning, while offering customization options to suit various dietary needs.

Chapter 2

Satisfying Soups and Stews

Introduction to Satisfying Soups and Stews

There's something undeniably comforting about a bowl of soup or stew, especially when it's been simmering for hours, allowing all the flavors to meld together beautifully. In this chapter, "Satisfying Soups and Stews," we'll explore a collection of hearty, nourishing recipes perfect for any season. Whether you're craving a classic Chicken Noodle Soup, a rich Beef and Barley Stew, or a creamy Tomato Basil Soup, these dishes are designed to be both simple and satisfying. Using your mini crock pot, you can create deeply flavorful meals with minimal effort, turning everyday ingredients into bowls of warmth and comfort that feed both body and soul.

Hearty Chicken Noodle Soup

broth. Using your mini crock pot, you can create this classic dish with ease, allowing the ingredients to meld together over time for a deeply satisfying soup that's sure to become a family favorite.

Preparation Time

- **Prep Time:** 15 minutes
- **Cooking Time:** 6-8 hours on low or 3-4 hours on high
- **Total Time:** 6 hours and 15 minutes to 8 hours and 15 minutes

Ingredients

- Chicken breasts (boneless, skinless): 2 medium (about 1 pound)
- Carrots (peeled and sliced): 2 large
- Celery stalks (sliced): 2 large
- Onion (diced): 1 medium
- Garlic (minced): 2 cloves
- Chicken broth (low sodium): 4 cups
- Water: 1 cup
- Dried thyme: 1 teaspoon
- Dried oregano: 1 teaspoon
- Bay leaf: 1 large
- Salt: 1 teaspoon (adjust to taste)
- Black pepper: ½ teaspoon (adjust to taste)
- Egg noodles: 1 ½ cups (uncooked)
- Fresh parsley (chopped one): 2 tablespoons (optional, for garnish)
- Lemon juice: 1 tablespoon (optional, for brightening the flavor)

Serving Size

Serves: 4

Procedure

1. **Prepare the Ingredients:** Start by prepping your vegetables. Peel and slice the carrots,

Hearty Chicken Noodle Soup is the ultimate comfort food, perfect for chilly days, when you're feeling under the weather, or simply when you crave something warm and nourishing. This recipe combines tender chicken, wholesome vegetables, and comforting noodles, all simmered together in a rich, flavorful

slice the celery stalks, dice the onion, and mince the garlic.

2. **Layer Ingredients in the Crock Pot:** In your mini crock pot (1.5 to 2.5 quarts), place the chicken breasts at the bottom. Add the sliced carrots, celery, diced onion, and minced garlic on top of the chicken. Sprinkle your dried thyme, dried oregano, salt, and the black pepper evenly over the vegetables.

3. **Add Liquids:** Pour the chicken broth and water over the ingredients in the crock pot. Stir gently to combine. Add the bay leaf on top.

4. **Cook:** Cover the crock pot with its lid and cook on low for 6–8 hours or on high for 3–4 hours, until the chicken is cooked through and the vegetables are tender.

5. **Shred the Chicken:** Once the chicken is fully cooked, remove it from the crock pot and place it on a cutting board. Using two forks, you should shred the chicken into bite-sized pieces, after that you return the shredded chicken to the crock pot and stir to combine.

6. **Add the Noodles:** About 20-30 minutes before serving, add the uncooked egg noodles to the crock pot. Stir them into the soup, cover, and continue cooking until the noodles are tender.

7. **Final Touches:** Before serving, remove the bay leaf and stir in the chopped fresh parsley and lemon juice, if using. These add a fresh, bright flavor to the soup.

8. **Serve:** Ladle the soup into bowls and serve warm. Enjoy with crusty bread or a side salad for a complete meal.

9. **Store and Reheat:** Leftovers can be stored in an airtight container in the refrigerator for up to 3 days. Reheat gently on the stove or in the microwave, adding a bit of extra broth or water if the soup has thickened.

Nutritional Value (Per Serving)

- **Calories:** Approximately 300 kcal
- **Protein:** 25g
- **Fat:** 7g
- **Carbohydrates:** 35g
- Fiber: 4g
- **Sugars:** 5g
- **Vitamin A:** 5500 IU
- **Vitamin C:** 15mg
- **Calcium:** 60mg
- **Iron:** 2.5mg

Cooking Tips

- **Use Bone-In Chicken:** For an even richer broth, you can use bone-in chicken breasts or thighs. Just be sure to remove the bones before shredding the chicken.

- **Customize the Noodles:** Egg noodles are traditional, but you can use any pasta you prefer, such as whole wheat or gluten-free noodles. Just adjust the cooking time as needed based on the type of pasta.

- **Control the Salt:** Start with less salt if you're using regular chicken broth instead of low sodium, as the salt content can vary widely between brands. And yes you can always add more salt later if needed.

- **Thicken the Broth:** If you prefer a thicker soup, you can make a slurry by mixing 1 tablespoon of cornstarch with 2 tablespoons of water and stirring it into the soup before adding the noodles. Let it cook for an additional 10-15 minutes to thicken.

- **Add Extra Vegetables:** Feel free to add other vegetables like peas, spinach, or diced potatoes. Just keep in mind that some vegetables may need more or less cooking time, so add them accordingly.

- **Brighten the Flavor:** A squeeze of fresh lemon juice added at the end of cooking brightens the flavor of the soup and enhances the overall taste, making it even more refreshing.

- **Freeze for Later:** Chicken Noodle Soup freezes well, but it's best to freeze it without the noodles, as they can become mushy when reheated. Simply cook the noodles fresh when you're ready to eat.

Health Benefits

- **High in Protein:** Chicken is an excellent source of lean protein, which is essential for muscle repair and growth, immune function, and overall body maintenance. A protein-rich soup like this helps keep you full and satisfied.

- **Rich in Vitamins and Minerals:** Listen, this very soup is packed with vegetables like carrots, celery, and onions, which provide the very essential vitamins and minerals. Carrots are really rich in vitamin A, which supports eye health, while celery is a good source of vitamin K and folate.

- **Boosts Immune System:** Chicken broth has long been touted for its immune-boosting properties, especially when you're feeling under the weather. The combination of warm broth, protein, and nutrient-dense vegetables makes this soup a powerful ally in fighting colds and flu.

- **Hydrating and Nourishing:** The broth in this soup helps to keep you hydrated, while the vegetables and chicken provide a nourishing, balanced meal. The combination of fluids, electrolytes, and nutrients is especially beneficial if you're recovering from illness.

- **Supports Digestive Health:** The vegetables in this soup are high in fiber, which supports healthy digestion and helps maintain a healthy gut microbiome. The broth itself is gentle on the digestive system, making this soup an excellent choice for those with sensitive stomachs.

- <u>Low in Calories:</u> This soup is relatively low in calories, making it a great option for those looking to maintain or lose weight while still enjoying a filling and satisfying meal.

- <u>Anti-Inflammatory:</u> Ingredients like garlic and onions contain compounds that have anti-inflammatory properties, which can help reduce inflammation in the body and promote overall health.

- <u>Heart-Healthy:</u> With its low fat and high vegetable content, this soup is heart-healthy. Using low-sodium broth and lean chicken further enhances its benefits for cardiovascular health.

Hearty Chicken Noodle Soup is a timeless classic that delivers comfort and nutrition in every bowl. By using your mini crock pot, you can easily prepare this wholesome dish, allowing the flavors to develop slowly and naturally. This recipe is perfect for those seeking a balanced, nourishing meal that's simple to make yet deeply satisfying. Whether you're looking to warm up on a cold day, recover from a cold, or simply enjoy a bowl of comfort, this Chicken Noodle Soup will be a go-to recipe in your kitchen.

Creamy Tomato Basil Soup

side of crusty bread or a grilled cheese sandwich, this soup is sure to warm both your body and soul. The slow cooking process involved here allows the flavors to meld together beautifully, resulting in a soup that's both satisfying and full of depth.

Preparation Time

- **Prep Time:** 15 minutes
- **Cooking Time:** 4–6 hours on low or 2–3 hours on high
- **Total Time:** 4 hours and 15 minutes to 6 hours and 15 minutes

Ingredients

- Canned whole tomatoes (with juice): 2 cans (28 ounces each)
- Vegetable broth (low sodium): 2 cups
- Onion (diced): 1 medium
- Carrots (peeled and chopped): 2 medium
- Garlic (minced): 3 cloves
- Fresh basil leaves: 1 cup (packed)
- Heavy cream: 1 cup (or coconut milk for a dairy-free option)
- Olive oil: 2 tablespoons
- Dried oregano: 1 teaspoon
- Dried thyme: 1 teaspoon
- Salt: 1 teaspoon (adjust to taste)
- Black pepper: ½ teaspoon (adjust to taste)
- Sugar: 1 tablespoon (optional, to balance acidity)
- Parmesan cheese (grated): Optional, for garnish
- Croutons or a drizzle of extra virgin olive oil: Optional, for garnish

Serving Size

Serves: 4–6

Procedure

Creamy Tomato Basil Soup is a rich and flavorful dish that combines the tanginess of ripe tomatoes with the aromatic sweetness of fresh basil, all brought together in a velvety, smooth base. This classic soup is comforting, nutritious, and incredibly easy to make using your mini crock pot. Whether you're serving it as a starter or enjoying it as a light meal with a

1. **Prepare the Vegetables:** Start by prepping your vegetables. Dice the onion, peel and chop the carrots, and mince the garlic.

2. **Sauté the Aromatics:** In a medium-sized skillet, heat the olive oil over medium heat. Add the diced onion and chopped carrots, sautéing for 5-7 minutes until the vegetables are soft and the onion is translucent. At this point, add the minced garlic and sauté for an additional minute until fragrant.

3. **Transfer to the Crock Pot:** Transfer the sautéed vegetables to your mini crock pot (1.5 to 2.5 quarts). Add the canned tomatoes (with their juice), vegetable broth, dried oregano, dried thyme, salt, and black pepper. Stir to combine all the ingredients.

4. **Cook:** Cover the crock pot with its lid and cook on low for 4–6 hours or on high for 2–3 hours, until the vegetables are very tender and the flavors have melded together.

5. **Blend the Soup:** Once the cooking time is up, use an immersion blender to carefully blend the soup directly in the crock pot until it is smooth and creamy. If you don't have an immersion blender, you can carefully transfer the soup to a countertop blender in batches, blending until smooth and then returning it to the crock pot.

6. **Add Cream and Basil:** Stir in the heavy cream (or coconut milk for a dairy-free option) and the fresh basil leaves. Continue cooking on low for an additional 15-20 minutes to allow the flavors to meld.

7. **Taste and Adjust Seasoning:** Taste the soup and adjust the seasoning as needed. If the tomatoes are particularly acidic, you can add a tablespoon of sugar to balance the flavors.

8. **Serve:** Ladle the soup into bowls and garnish with grated Parmesan cheese, croutons, or a drizzle of extra virgin olive oil, if desired. Serve warm with a side of crusty bread or a grilled cheese sandwich for a complete meal.

9. **Store and Reheat:** Leftovers can be stored in an airtight container in the refrigerator for up to 3 days. You can reheat gently on the stove or maybe in the microwave until warmed through.

Nutritional Value (Per Serving, Based on 6 Servings)

- **Calories:** Approximately 180 kcal
- **Protein:** 4g
- **Fat:** 12g
- **Carbohydrates:** 18g
- **Fiber:** 4g
- **Sugars:** 9g
- **Vitamin A:** 4500 IU
- **Vitamin C:** 20mg
- **Calcium:** 80mg
- **Iron:** 2mg

Cooking Tips

- **Choose Quality Tomatoes:** The soup's flavor hinges on good tomatoes. Opt for high-quality canned tomatoes like San Marzano for their sweetness and low acidity.

- **Creamier Texture:** For a richer soup, increase the heavy cream or use half-and-half. For a lighter option, try evaporated milk or more vegetable broth.

- **Balance Acidity:** If the soup tastes too acidic, add sugar—start with a teaspoon and adjust to your preference.

- **Dairy-Free Option:** Swap heavy cream with coconut milk or cashew cream for a dairy-free version that's still creamy.

- **Boost Flavor:** A splash of balsamic vinegar or hot sauce at the end of cooking can deepen the soup's flavor.

- **Add Protein:** For a heartier soup, mix in cooked chickpeas, white beans, or shredded chicken.

- **Creative Garnishes:** Beyond Parmesan and croutons, try pesto, red pepper flakes, or flavored olive oil for extra flavor.

- **Perfect Pairing:** This soup pairs well with grilled cheese or a fresh green salad for a balanced meal.

Health Benefits

- **Antioxidant-Rich:** Tomatoes are loaded with lycopene, which helps reduce the risk of chronic diseases.

- **Immune Support:** Vitamin C from tomatoes and carrots boosts immune function.

- **Heart Health:** Basil and olive oil offer heart-healthy fats and antioxidants, which can lower cholesterol and reduce inflammation.

- **Fiber-Rich:** The soup provides dietary fiber from tomatoes and carrots, aiding digestion and supporting gut health.

- **Supports Vision:** High in vitamin A, this soup helps maintain healthy vision.

- **Low-Calorie:** Despite its creamy texture, this soup is low in calories, making it a light yet satisfying option.

- **Anti-Inflammatory:** Tomatoes and basil have anti-inflammatory properties that support overall health.

- **Hydrating:** With its high water content and broth base, this soup helps maintain hydration.

Creamy Tomato Basil Soup is a comforting, nutrient-packed dish that's simple to prepare. With your mini crock pot, you can easily create a flavorful, creamy soup perfect for any meal. Enjoy it with crusty bread or grilled cheese for a nourishing, indulgent experience.

Beef and Barley Stew

flavors to meld together over time for a stew that's deeply flavorful and fulfilling. Whether you're serving it as a weeknight dinner or preparing it for a cozy weekend meal, this Beef and Barley Stew is sure to be a hit.

Preparation Time

- **Prep Time:** 20 minutes
- **Cooking Time:** 6–8 hours on low or 3–4 hours on high
- **Total Time:** 6 hours and 20 minutes to 8 hours and 20 minutes

Ingredients

- Beef chuck roast (cut into 1-inch cubes): 1 pound
- Pearl barley: ½ cup (uncooked)
- Carrots (peeled and chopped): 2 medium
- Celery stalks (chopped): 2 medium
- Onion (diced): 1 large
- Garlic (minced): 3 cloves
- Mushrooms (sliced): 1 cup
- Beef broth (low sodium): 4 cups
- Tomato paste: 2 tablespoons
- Worcestershire sauce: 1 tablespoon
- Bay leaf: 1 large
- Dried thyme: 1 teaspoon
- Dried rosemary: 1 teaspoon
- Salt: 1 teaspoon (adjust to taste)
- Black pepper: ½ teaspoon (adjust to taste)
- Olive oil: 2 tablespoons
- Fresh parsley (chopped one): 2 tablespoons (optional, for garnish)

Serving Size

Serves: 4–6

Procedure

Beef and Barley Stew is the epitome of comfort food, offering a hearty, satisfying meal that's perfect for cold days or whenever you're in the mood for something robust and nourishing. This stew is rich in flavor, featuring tender chunks of beef, earthy vegetables, and nutty barley, all simmered together in a savory broth. Using your mini crock pot, you can easily prepare this dish with minimal effort, allowing the

1. **Prepare the Ingredients:** Start by prepping your vegetables. Peel and chop the carrots, chop the celery, dice the onion, slice the mushrooms, and mince the garlic. Cut the beef chuck roast into 1-inch cubes, trimming any excess fat.

2. **Brown the Beef:** Now in a large skillet, heat the olive oil over medium-high heat. Add the beef cubes in a single layer, working in batches if necessary to avoid overcrowding the pan. Brown the beef on all sides, about 4–5 minutes per batch, until a deep golden crust forms. Transfer the browned beef to your mini crock pot (1.5 to 2.5 quarts).

3. **Sauté the Vegetables:** In the same skillet, add the diced onion, chopped carrots, celery, and mushrooms. Sauté for about 5–7 minutes until the vegetables are softened and you see the onions become translucent. Add the minced garlic and cook for an additional minute until fragrant.

4. **Deglaze the Pan:** Add the tomato paste and Worcestershire sauce to the skillet with the vegetables. Stir to combine and cook for 1-2 minutes. Then, pour in about ½ cup of the beef broth, scraping up any browned bits from the bottom of the skillet (this adds extra flavor). Transfer this mixture to the crock pot with the beef.

5. **Add Remaining Ingredients:** Add the pearl barley, dried thyme, dried rosemary, bay leaf, salt, and pepper to the crock pot. Pour in the remaining beef broth, ensuring all ingredients are submerged. Stir to combine.

6. **Cook:** Cover the crock pot with its lid and cook on low for 6–8 hours or on high for 3-4 hours, until the beef is tender, the barley is cooked, and the flavors have melded together.

7. **Finish and Serve:** Before serving, remove the bay leaf and taste the stew, adjusting the seasoning with more salt and pepper if needed. If the stew is too thick, you can thin it with a little more broth or water. Ladle the stew into bowls and garnish with fresh chopped parsley if desired. Serve warm, with crusty bread or a side salad, whichever you prefer.

8. **Store and Reheat:** Leftovers can be stored in an airtight container in the refrigerator for up to 3 days. Reheat gently on the stove or in the microwave, adding a bit of extra broth if the stew has thickened.

Nutritional Value (Per Serving, Based on 6 Servings)

- **Calories:** Approximately 350 kcal
- **Protein:** 25g
- **Fat:** 15g
- **Carbohydrates:** 30g
- **Fiber:** 6g
- **Sugars:** 4g
- **Vitamin A:** 4000 IU
- **Vitamin C:** 10mg
- **Calcium:** 60mg

- Iron: 4mg

Cooking Tips

1. **Best Cut:** Use chuck roast for its marbling, or try short ribs or brisket for tender, flavorful meat.

2. **Brown the Beef:** Browning adds a rich crust and depth to the stew's flavor.

3. **Barley Choices:** Use pearl barley for quick cooking or hulled barley for a whole-grain option, though it cooks longer.

4. **Consistency Control:** Barley thickens the stew, so add extra broth if you prefer it thinner.

5. **Add Veggies Later:** To keep vegetables firm, add them halfway through cooking.

6. **Flavor Boost:** Enhance the stew with red wine, balsamic vinegar, or soy sauce.

7. **Freezing Tip:** Freeze the stew without barley to avoid mushiness; add freshly cooked barley when reheating.

Health Benefits

- **High in Protein:** Beef provides essential protein for muscle repair and metabolism.

- **Rich in Fiber:** Barley offers soluble fiber that lowers cholesterol and aids digestion.

- **Nutrient-Dense:** The stew is packed with vitamins and minerals like vitamin A and iron.

- **Heart Healthy:** Barley helps reduce cholesterol and improves blood pressure.

- **Immune Support:** Garlic, onions, and veggies boost immunity and reduce inflammation.

- **Digestive Health:** Fiber from barley and vegetables promotes healthy digestion.

- **Anti-Inflammatory:** Herbs like rosemary and thyme help reduce inflammation.

- **Energy Sustaining:** The mix of protein, fiber, and carbs provides lasting energy.

- **Low in Fat:** Using lean beef and minimal oil keeps this stew hearty yet low in fat.

Beef and Barley Stew is a hearty, nutritious dish perfect for any season. With tender beef, wholesome barley, and vegetables simmered slowly in a flavorful broth, it's a satisfying meal made easy with your mini crock pot. Ideal for family meals or meal prep, this stew offers rich flavors and balanced nutrition with minimal effort.

Hearty Chicken and Vegetable Stew

with tender chicken, flavorful vegetables, and aromatic herbs, this stew is both satisfying and healthy, providing a great balance of protein, fiber, and essential vitamins.

Preparation Time

- **Prep Time:** 10 minutes
- **Cook Time:** 4-5 hours on low

Serving size

Servings: 2

Ingredients:

- 2 boneless, skinless chicken thighs (or 1 chicken breast), diced
- 1 small potato, peeled and diced
- 1 carrot, peeled and sliced
- 1 celery stalk, diced
- ½ small onion, diced
- 1 clove garlic, minced
- ½ cup low-sodium chicken broth
- ½ cup diced tomatoes (canned or fresh)
- ½ teaspoon dried thyme
- ½ teaspoon dried rosemary
- 1 bay leaf
- Salt and pepper to taste
- 1 tablespoon olive oil (optional for browning chicken)
- Fresh parsley for garnish (optional)

Procedure:

1. **Optional Browning:** For more flavor, brown the diced chicken in olive oil over medium heat for 3-4 minutes. Lightly season with salt and pepper.

2. **Prep the Vegetables:** Dice the potatoes, carrots, celery, onion, and garlic.

The Mini Crock Pot Hearty Chicken and Vegetable Stew is a nutritious and filling meal, perfect for cold days or when you're craving a comforting, homemade dish. Packed

3. **Combine Ingredients:** Add the chicken, potatoes, carrots, celery, onion, garlic, chicken broth, tomatoes, thyme, rosemary, and bay leaf to the mini crock pot. Stir to combine.

4. **Cook:** Cover and cook on low for 4-5 hours, or until the vegetables are tender and the chicken is fully cooked.

5. **Finish:** Remove the bay leaf, season with salt and pepper to taste, and garnish with fresh parsley if desired.

6. **Serve:** Ladle the stew into bowls and serve them warm. Pair with crusty bread or a side salad for a heartier meal.

Nutritional Value (Per Serving):

- **Calories:** ~320
- **Protein:** ~28g
- **Fat:** ~10g
- **Carbohydrates:** ~30g
- **Fiber:** ~6g
- **Vitamins & Minerals:** Rich in vitamin A, vitamin C, potassium, and iron.

Cooking Tips:

- **Use Chicken Thighs:** Chicken thighs are juicier and more flavorful, but chicken breast can be used for a leaner option.

- **Customize Vegetables:** Add your favorite vegetables like zucchini, green beans, or bell peppers for added nutrients.

- **Thicken the Stew:** For a thicker consistency, remove ¼ cup of broth, mix with a teaspoon of cornstarch or flour, and stir it back into the stew. Cook on high for another good 15 minutes.

- **Make Ahead:** Prep the ingredients the night before for easy assembly in the morning.

Health Benefits:

- **High in Protein:** Chicken provides lean protein, essential for muscle repair, immune function, and maintaining energy levels throughout the day.

- **Rich in Vitamins:** Vegetables like carrots and tomatoes supply vitamins A and C, which boost immunity, support vision, and promote skin health.

- **Gut-Friendly Fiber:** Potatoes and carrots offer a good amount of fiber, promoting digestion and helping you feel full longer.

- **Low-Calorie, Filling Meal:** This stew is low in calories but filling, making it ideal for weight management or as part of a balanced diet.

- **Heart-Healthy Fats:** Olive oil is a great source of monounsaturated fats, which can reduce inflammation and support heart health.

- **Anti-Inflammatory Herbs:** Thyme and rosemary not only add flavor but also provide anti-inflammatory and antioxidant benefits, promoting overall wellness.

This Mini Crock Pot Hearty Chicken and Vegetable Stew is a simple, wholesome meal that delivers comfort and nutrition in every bite. With lean protein, fiber-rich vegetables, and heart-healthy ingredients, it's a perfect choice for those looking for a healthy, filling, and flavorful stew.

Creamy Lentil and Spinach Soup

healthy. It's easy to prepare and full of bold flavors from spices like cumin and turmeric.

Preparation Time

- **Prep Time**: 10 minutes
- **Cook Time**: 4-5 hours on low

Serving Size

- Servings: 2

Ingredients:

- ½ cup dried green or brown lentils, rinsed
- 2 cups low-sodium vegetable broth
- 1 cup water
- 1 small onion, diced
- 1 carrot, peeled and diced
- 1 celery stalk, diced
- 2 garlic cloves, minced
- ½ teaspoon ground cumin
- ½ teaspoon ground turmeric
- ¼ teaspoon smoked paprika
- Salt and pepper to taste
- 2 cups fresh spinach, chopped
- ½ cup canned coconut milk (or any plant-based milk)
- 1 tablespoon lemon juice (optional)
- Fresh cilantro for garnish (optional)

Procedure:

1. **Rinse the Lentils:** Thoroughly rinse lentils under cold water.

2. **Combine Ingredients:** Add the rinsed lentils, onion, carrot, celery, garlic, vegetable broth, water, cumin, turmeric,

The Slow-Cooker Creamy Lentil and Spinach Soup is a comforting, nutrient-rich meal, perfect for lunch or dinner. This plant-based soup is loaded with protein from lentils, fiber from vegetables, and a creamy texture from coconut milk, making it both satisfying and

smoked paprika, salt, and pepper to the mini crock pot. Stir well.

3. <u>Cook:</u> Cover and cook on low for 4-5 hours, or until lentils and vegetables are tender.

4. <u>Add Spinach and Coconut Milk:</u> Stir in the chopped spinach and coconut milk. Cook for an additional 20-30 minutes until the spinach wilts and the soup becomes creamy.

5. <u>Blend (Optional):</u> For a smoother texture, blend part of the soup with an immersion blender, or blend half the soup and mix it back in.

6. <u>Finish:</u> Stir in the lemon juice, adjust seasoning, and garnish with cilantro if desired. Serve warm.

Nutritional Value (Per Serving):

- <u>Calories:</u> ~280
- <u>Protein:</u> ~12g
- <u>Fat:</u> ~10g
- <u>Carbohydrates:</u> ~34g
- <u>Fiber:</u> ~13g
- <u>Vitamins & Minerals:</u> Rich in iron, folate, vitamin A, vitamin C, and potassium.

Cooking Tips:

- <u>Adjust Texture:</u> Blend all or part of the soup for a creamier texture, or leave it chunky for a heartier bite.

- <u>Add Protein:</u> For extra protein, stir in chickpeas or serve with a dollop of yogurt.

- <u>Flavor Boost:</u> Add red pepper flakes for heat, or a sprinkle of nutritional yeast or parmesan for umami flavor.

- <u>Meal Prep:</u> This soup can be stored in the fridge for up to 4 days or frozen for 3 months.

Health Benefits:

- <u>High in Protein:</u> Lentils provide plant-based protein, essential for muscle repair and energy production, making this soup ideal for vegetarians and vegans.

- <u>Rich in Fiber:</u> Lentils and vegetables contribute fiber, aiding digestion, regulating blood sugar, and keeping you full longer.

- <u>Boosts Iron:</u> Lentils are rich in iron, vital for oxygen transport in the body. Paired with spinach, which enhances iron absorption, this soup helps maintain healthy energy levels.

- <u>Heart-Healthy Fats:</u> Coconut milk adds healthy fats that support brain function and reduce inflammation, while keeping the soup dairy-free.

- **Low-Calorie, Nutrient-Dense:** Despite being low in calories, this soup is loaded with vitamins A and C from spinach, which support immunity and skin health.

- **Anti-Inflammatory Spices:** Cumin and turmeric have powerful anti-inflammatory properties, promoting overall wellness and reducing inflammation in the body.

The Slow-Cooker Creamy Lentil and Spinach Soup is a wholesome, easy-to-make meal, perfect for meal prep or a quick weeknight dinner. Packed with plant-based protein, fiber, and essential nutrients, it's a flavorful, nutritious option for anyone looking for a healthy and filling soup.

<u>Congratulations! You've Made It Through Two Delicious Chapters!</u>

If you're reading this, you've already dived into the world of mouthwatering breakfasts and hearty soups and stews from this book. I hope you're feeling inspired, nourished, and excited to keep cooking with your trusty mini Crock Pot!

Before we move on to even more exciting recipes, I'd love to hear how you're enjoying the book so far. Your honest feedback is incredibly valuable—it helps me improve and ensures others can make the most of this cookbook too. If you're willing, please take a moment to share your thoughts by leaving a review on Amazon.

Whether you've tried one recipe or ten, your review makes a huge difference. Thank you for being part of this journey, and I can't wait for you to explore the rest of the book!

Happy cooking!

Chapter 3

Simple Suppers

Introduction to Simple Suppers

After a long day, there's nothing better than sitting down to a delicious, home-cooked meal that didn't require hours of preparation. In "Simple Suppers," we've gathered a collection of easy, satisfying recipes that are perfect for dinner any night of the week. These dishes are designed to be both flavorful and straightforward, allowing you to create wholesome, comforting meals with minimal effort. Whether you're in the mood for juicy Pulled BBQ Chicken, tender Lemon Herb Chicken, or a hearty Three-Bean Chili, these recipes are sure to become your go-to choices for quick and nourishing suppers that everyone will love.

Pulled BBQ Chicken

Pulled BBQ Chicken is a flavorful, tender dish that's perfect for those who crave the rich, smoky taste of barbecue without spending hours at the grill. This recipe uses your mini crock pot to slowly cook chicken breasts until they're perfectly tender and infused with a sweet and tangy BBQ sauce. The result is juicy, shredded chicken that's incredibly versatile—you can serve it on sandwich buns, over rice, in tacos, or alongside your favorite sides. It's an easy, hands-off meal that's ideal for busy weeknights, casual gatherings, or meal prepping for the week.

Preparation Time

- **Prep Time:** 10 minutes
- **Cooking Time:** 4–6 hours on low or 2–3 hours on high
- **Total Time:** 4 hours and 10 minutes to 6 hours and 10 minutes

Ingredients

- Chicken breasts (boneless, skinless): 1 ½ pounds (about 3-4 medium breasts)
- BBQ sauce: 1 cup (homemade or your favorite store-bought)
- Onion (finely chopped): 1 small
- Garlic (minced): 2 cloves
- Apple cider vinegar: 2 tablespoons
- Brown sugar: 2 tablespoons (optional, for added sweetness)
- Smoked paprika: 1 teaspoon
- Worcestershire sauce: 1 tablespoon
- Salt: ½ teaspoon (adjust to taste)
- Black pepper: ½ teaspoon (adjust to taste)
- Olive oil: 1 tablespoon (optional, for sautéing the onion and garlic)
- Buns: For serving (optional)
- Coleslaw: For topping (optional)

Serving Size

Serves: 4–6

Procedure

1. **Prepare the Chicken**: Start by trimming any excess fat from the chicken breasts and patting them dry with paper towels. Now season the chicken with salt and pepper on both sides.

2. **Sauté the Onion and Garlic (Optional):** In a small skillet, heat the olive oil over medium heat. Add the finely chopped onion and sauté for 3-4 minutes until softened and translucent. Next, add the minced garlic and cook for an additional minute until fragrant. This step is optional but helps to deepen the flavor of the dish.

3. **Combine Ingredients in the Crock Pot:** In your mini crock pot (1.5 to 2.5 quarts), add the BBQ sauce, apple cider vinegar, brown sugar (if using), smoked paprika, Worcestershire sauce, and the sautéed onion and garlic mixture. Stir to combine.

4. **Add the Chicken:** Place the seasoned chicken breasts into the BBQ sauce mixture in the crock pot, turning them to coat fully. And yes, make sure that the chicken is submerged in the sauce.

5. **Cook:** Cover the crock pot with its lid and cook on low for 4-6 hours or on high for 2-3 hours, until the chicken is tender and easily shredded with a fork.

6. **Shred the Chicken:** Once the chicken is cooked, remove it from the crock pot and place it on a cutting board. Go ahead to use two forks to shred the chicken into bite-sized pieces.

7. **Return to the Sauce:** Return the shredded chicken to the crock pot and stir it into the sauce, ensuring all the chicken is evenly coated. Let it cook for an additional 15-20 minutes on low to allow the flavors to meld.

8. **Serve:** Serve the pulled BBQ chicken on sandwich buns topped with coleslaw, over rice, in tacos, or as part of a BBQ platter with sides like corn on the cob and potato salad.

9. **Store and Reheat:** Leftovers can be stored in an airtight container in the refrigerator for up to 3 days. Reheat gently in the microwave or on the stove, adding a little extra BBQ sauce or water if needed to keep it moist.

Nutritional Value (Per Serving, Based on 6 Servings)

- **Calories:** Approximately 250 kcal
- **Protein:** 27g
- **Fat:** 7g
- **Carbohydrates:** 20g
- **Fiber:** 1g
- **Sugars:** 15g (varies based on the BBQ sauce used)

- **Vitamin A:** 500 IU
- **Vitamin C:** 2mg
- **Calcium:** 20mg
- **Iron:** 1mg

Cooking Tips

- **Use Chicken Thighs:** For juicier, more flavorful results, opt for boneless, skinless chicken thighs instead of breasts.

- **Customize BBQ Sauce:** Choose or create a BBQ sauce that matches your taste—smoky, sweet, or spicy. Experiment with regional styles like Carolina mustard or Kansas City sauce.

- **Simplify Prep:** Skip sautéing the onion and garlic if you're short on time. Adding them raw will still infuse the dish with flavor as they cook.

- **Add Smokiness:** For a smoky flavor, add a teaspoon of liquid smoke to the crock pot.

- **Thicken the Sauce:** If the sauce is too thin, cook uncovered for 15-20 minutes or stir in a cornstarch slurry.

- **Double for Meal Prep:** Easily double the recipe for meal prepping or feeding a crowd. Ensure your crock pot can handle the volume.

- **Versatile Serving:** Serve on buns with coleslaw, over a baked potato, or in tacos. Pair with sides like corn on the cob or a fresh salad.

Health Benefits

- **High in Protein:** Chicken provides lean protein, essential for muscle growth and maintenance, keeping you full and satisfied.

- **Low in Fat:** Using chicken breasts keeps the dish low in fat, making it a heart-healthy option without sacrificing flavor.

- **Immune Support:** Garlic and onions boost immunity with antioxidants and anti-inflammatory compounds.

- **Balanced Meal:** Pair with whole grains and vegetables for a nutrient-rich, complete meal.

- **Energy Boost:** The protein and carbs provide sustained energy, perfect for an active lifestyle.

- **Diet-Friendly:** Adapt the recipe for various diets by using sugar-free or gluten-free BBQ sauce.

- **<u>Mindful Eating:</u>** Cooking at home lets you control ingredients and portions, promoting healthier eating habits.

Pulled BBQ Chicken is a flavorful, easy-to-make dish ideal for any occasion. With minimal prep and the convenience of a mini crock pot, you can enjoy tender, protein-rich chicken in a variety of ways. Whether in sandwiches, over rice, or in tacos, this dish is sure to be a household favorite

Garlic Herb Pork Tenderloin

it an ideal centerpiece for a variety of meals. Whether you're hosting a dinner party or preparing a simple weeknight dinner, this dish is both impressive and easy to make. The result is a succulent, mouth-watering pork tenderloin that pairs wonderfully with a variety of sides, from roasted vegetables to mashed potatoes.

Preparation Time

- **Prep Time:** 15 minutes
- **Cooking Time:** 3–4 hours on low or 1.5–2 hours on high
- **Total Time:** 3 hours and 15 minutes to 4 hours and 15 minutes

Ingredients

- Pork tenderloin: 1–1.5 pounds
- Garlic (minced): 4 cloves
- Fresh rosemary (chopped): 1 tablespoon
- Fresh thyme (chopped): 1 tablespoon
- Fresh parsley (chopped): 2 tablespoons
- Lemon zest: 1 teaspoon
- Olive oil: 2 tablespoons
- Salt: 1 teaspoon (adjust to taste)
- Black pepper: ½ teaspoon (adjust to taste)
- Chicken broth (low sodium): ½ cup
- Lemon juice: 1 tablespoon
- Honey or maple syrup: 1 tablespoon (optional, for a touch of sweetness)
- Dijon mustard: 1 tablespoon (optional, for extra flavor)

Serving Size

Serves: 4

Procedure

Garlic Herb Pork Tenderloin is a beautifully seasoned dish that combines the tenderness of pork with the aromatic flavors of garlic, fresh herbs, and a hint of citrus. Slow-cooked to perfection in your mini crock pot, this pork tenderloin becomes incredibly juicy and flavorful, making

1. **Prepare the Pork Tenderloin**: Start this by trimming any excess fat or silver skin from the pork tenderloin you have. Pat the tenderloin dry with paper towels to ensure a good sear.

2. **Make the Garlic Herb Rub:** In your small bowl, combine the minced garlic, chopped rosemary, thyme, parsley, lemon zest, salt, and black pepper. Add the olive oil and mix until it forms a paste-like consistency.

3. **Season the Pork:** Rub the garlic herb mixture all over the pork tenderloin, ensuring it's evenly coated. If possible, let the pork sit for 10-15 minutes to allow the flavors to penetrate the meat.

4. **Sear the Pork (Optional):** For added flavor, you can sear the pork tenderloin in a hot skillet before placing it in the crock pot. eat a tablespoon of olive oil in a large skillet over medium-high heat. Then sear the pork on all sides until it develops a golden-brown crust, about 2-3 minutes per side. This step is optional but enhances the depth of flavor.

5. **Place in the Crock Pot:** Transfer the seasoned (and seared, if done) pork tenderloin to your mini crock pot (1.5 to 2.5 quarts).

6. **Add Liquid**: In a small bowl, whisk together the chicken broth, lemon juice, honey or maple syrup (if using), and Dijon mustard (if using). Pour this mixture over the pork tenderloin in the crock pot.

7. **Cook:** Cover the crock pot with its lid and cook on low for 3-4 hours or on high for 1.5-2 hours, until the pork is tender and reaches an internal temperature of 145°F (63°C).

8. **Rest and Slice:** Once the pork is cooked, remove it from the crock pot and let it rest on a cutting board for 5-10 minutes before slicing. Resting allows the juices to redistribute, keeping the meat tender and juicy.

9. **Serve:** Slice the pork tenderloin into medallions and drizzle with the remaining sauce from the crock pot. Serve warm with your choice of sides, such as roasted vegetables, mashed potatoes, or a fresh salad.

10. **Store and Reheat:** Leftovers can be stored in an airtight container in the refrigerator for up to 3 days. Reheat gently in the microwave or on the stove, adding a splash of broth to keep the pork moist.

Nutritional Value (Per Serving, Based on 4 Servings)

- **Calories:** Approximately 250 kcal
- **Protein:** 28g

- **Fat:** 14g
- **Carbohydrates:** 3g
- **Fiber:** 0g
- **Sugars:** 2g
- **Vitamin C:** 5mg
- **Iron:** 1.5mg
- **Calcium:** 30mg

Cooking Tips

- **Choose the Right Pork:** Pork tenderloin is lean and tender, perfect for slow cooking. For a richer flavor, try pork loin, but adjust cooking times.

- **Sear for Flavor:** Searing adds depth, creating a caramelized crust that enhances the dish. It's an optional but worthwhile step.

- **Use Fresh Herbs:** Fresh rosemary, thyme, and parsley offer the best flavor, if using dried herbs, use half the amount.

- **Adjust Sweetness:** Honey or maple syrup adds balance. Omit for a savory dish or increase for more sweetness.

- **Thicken the Sauce:** To thicken, simmer the sauce after removing the pork or stir in a cornstarch slurry.

- **Check Doneness:** Use a meat thermometer to ensure the pork reaches 145°F (63°C) to prevent dryness.

- **Pairing Suggestions:** Pairs well with sides like garlic mashed potatoes, roasted Brussels sprouts, or quinoa salad.

- **Meal Prep Friendly:** Slice and store portions for easy, balanced meals throughout the week.

Health Benefits

- **High in Protein:** Pork tenderloin provides lean protein essential for muscle repair and metabolism.

- **Low in Fat:** This lean cut keeps the dish low in fat, perfect for a healthier diet.

- **Rich in Nutrients:** Provides B vitamins for energy and zinc for immune health.

- **Heart Healthy:** Olive oil, fresh herbs, and lemon juice contribute to heart health with healthy fats and antioxidants.

- **Supports Digestion:** Garlic and herbs aid digestion and support gut health.

- **Boosts Immunity:** Garlic, herbs, and lemon juice strengthen the immune system.

- **Anti-Inflammatory:** Rosemary and thyme help reduce inflammation and promote overall health.

- **Versatile Dish:** Balanced in flavor and nutrition, it pairs well with various sides for different dietary needs.

Garlic Herb Pork Tenderloin is a flavorful, easy-to-make dish perfect for any occasion. The mini crock pot ensures tender, juicy pork infused with fresh garlic and herbs. With high protein, low fat, and a wealth of nutrients, this dish supports a healthy diet while delighting your taste buds. Whether for a quick dinner or a meal to impress guests, this recipe is sure to become a favorite.

Three-Bean Chili

meld together beautifully, resulting in a rich and robust chili that will warm you from the inside out. Whether you're looking for a meatless meal option or simply want to enjoy a delicious bowl of chili, this recipe is sure to become a staple in your kitchen.

Preparation Time

- **Prep Time:** 15 minutes
- **Cooking Time:** 6–8 hours on low or 3–4 hours on high
- **Total Time:** 6 hours and 15 minutes to 8 hours and 15 minutes

Ingredients

- Kidney beans (canned, drained and rinsed): 1 can (15 ounces)
- Black beans (canned, drained and rinsed): 1 can (15 ounces)
- Pinto beans (canned, drained and rinsed): 1 can (15 ounces)
- Onion (diced): 1 large
- Bell pepper (diced): 1 large (any color)
- Carrots (peeled and chopped): 2 medium
- Garlic (minced): 4 cloves
- Canned diced tomatoes (with juice): 2 cans (14.5 ounces each)
- Tomato paste: 2 tablespoons
- Vegetable broth (low sodium): 1 cup
- Chili powder: 2 tablespoons
- Ground cumin: 2 teaspoons
- Smoked paprika: 1 teaspoon
- Dried oregano: 1 teaspoon
- Ground coriander: 1 teaspoon
- Cayenne pepper: ¼ teaspoon (optional, for heat)
- Salt: 1 teaspoon (adjust to taste)

Three-Bean Chili is a hearty, nutritious, and flavorful dish that's perfect for any occasion, from a cozy family dinner to a casual gathering with friends. This vegetarian chili is packed with protein and fiber from three types of beans, making it both filling and satisfying. The slow-cooking process allows the flavors of the spices, tomatoes, and beans to

- Black pepper: ½ teaspoon (adjust to taste)
- Olive oil: 2 tablespoons
- Bay leaf: 1 large
- Fresh cilantro (chopped): ¼ cup (optional, for garnish)
- Lime wedges: For serving (optional)
- Sour cream, shredded cheese, and avocado: Optional toppings

Serving Size

Serves: 6

Procedure

1. <u>Prepare the Vegetables:</u> Start by dicing the onion and bell pepper, peeling and chopping the carrots, and mincing the garlic.

2. <u>Sauté the Vegetables (Optional):</u> In a large skillet, heat the olive oil over medium heat. Add the diced onion, bell pepper, and carrots. Sauté for 5–7 minutes, until the vegetables are softened and the onion is translucent. Then add the minced garlic and cook for an additional minute until fragrant, this step helps to deepen the flavor of the chili but can be skipped if you're short on time.

3. <u>Combine Ingredients in the Crock Pot</u>: Transfer the sautéed vegetables to your mini crock pot (1.5 to 2.5 quarts). Add the drained and rinsed kidney beans, black beans, and pinto beans. Stir in the diced tomatoes (with their juice), tomato paste, vegetable broth, chili powder, ground cumin, smoked paprika, dried oregano, ground coriander, cayenne pepper (if using), salt, black pepper, and the bay leaf. Stir everything together until well combined.

4. <u>Cook:</u> Cover the crock pot with its lid and cook on low for 6–8 hours or on high for 3–4 hours, until the vegetables are tender and the flavors have melded together.

5. <u>Adjust Seasoning:</u> After cooking, remove the bay leaf and taste the chili. You then adjust the seasoning with more salt, pepper, or spices if needed.

6. <u>Serve:</u> Ladle the chili into bowls and garnish with chopped fresh cilantro and a squeeze of lime juice for added freshness. You can also top your chili with sour cream, shredded cheese, avocado, or any of your favorite toppings.

7. <u>Store and Reheat:</u> Leftovers can be stored in an airtight container in the refrigerator for up to 4 days. You can reheat gently on the stove or in the microwave until warmed through. This chili also freezes well for up to 3 months.

Nutritional Value (Per Serving, Based on 6 Servings)

- Calories: Approximately 280 kcal

- Protein: 13g
- Fat: 6g
- Carbohydrates: 45g
- Fiber: 13g
- Sugars: 8g
- Vitamin A: 8000 IU
- Vitamin C: 40mg
- Calcium: 100mg
- Iron: 5mg

Cooking Tips

1. **Customize Your Beans:** Mix and match beans like cannellini, navy, or chickpeas for varied textures and flavors.

2. **Add Smokiness:** For a smoky kick, add a chopped chipotle in adobo sauce; adjust cayenne for heat.

3. **Thicken the Chili:** Remove the lid in the last 30 minutes or mash some beans to thicken naturally.

4. **Boost Veggies:** Add zucchini, corn, or spinach for extra nutrition.

5. **Increase Protein:** Add quinoa, bulgur, or tofu for more protein without meat.

6. **Adjust Spice:** Modify the cayenne to control heat, or add hot sauce when serving.

7. **Serving Suggestions:** Serve with cornbread, over baked potatoes, or with brown rice. Top with cheese, sour cream, or avocado.

Health Benefits

- **High Fiber:** Beans provide fiber for digestion, blood sugar regulation, and lowering cholesterol.

- **Plant-Based Protein:** A great vegetarian protein source for muscle repair and immune function.

- **Nutrient-Rich:** Packed with vitamins and minerals from vegetables like bell peppers and tomatoes.

- **Heart Health:** High in fiber and low in saturated fat, promoting a healthy heart.

- **Blood Sugar Control:** Fiber helps stabilize blood sugar, ideal for managing diabetes.

- **Promotes Fullness:** Protein and fiber keep you full, aiding in weight management.

- **Anti-Inflammatory:** Spices like chili powder and cumin reduce inflammation.

- **Immune Support:** Garlic, onions, and peppers boost immunity with antioxidants.

- **Low-Calorie:** Filling yet low in calories, perfect for those watching their intake.

Three-Bean Chili is a nutritious, flavorful dish perfect for any time of year. Versatile and adaptable, it suits various tastes and dietary needs. Whether for a weeknight dinner, meal prep, or feeding a crowd, this chili offers a healthy, satisfying meal packed with protein, fiber, and essential nutrients.

Lemon Herb Chicken

with vibrant flavors. It's an ideal recipe for those seeking a light yet satisfying meal that's both healthy and easy to prepare. Whether served with a side of roasted vegetables, over a bed of rice, or in a salad, Lemon Herb Chicken is a versatile dish that will quickly become a staple in your meal rotation.

Preparation Time

- **Prep Time:** 15 minutes
- **Cooking Time:** 4–6 hours on low or 2–3 hours on high
- **Total Time:** 4 hours and 15 minutes to 6 hours and 15 minutes

Ingredients

- Chicken breasts (boneless, skinless): 1 ½ pounds (about 3-4 medium breasts)
- Fresh lemon juice: ¼ cup (juice of about 2 lemons)
- Lemon zest: 1 teaspoon
- Garlic (minced): 4 cloves
- Fresh rosemary (chopped): 1 tablespoon
- Fresh thyme (chopped): 1 tablespoon
- Fresh parsley (chopped): 2 tablespoons
- Olive oil: 2 tablespoons
- Chicken broth (low sodium): ½ cup
- Honey: One (1) tablespoon (optional, for a touch of sweetness)
- Salt: 1 teaspoon (adjust to taste)
- Black pepper: ½ teaspoon (adjust to taste)
- Optional Garnish: Additional lemon slices and fresh herbs

Serving Size

Serves: 4

The Lemon Herb Chicken is a very fresh and flavorful dish that combines the zesty brightness of lemon with the aromatic essence of fresh herbs. Slow-cooked to perfection in your mini crock pot, this chicken is incredibly tender, juicy, and infused

Procedure

1. **Prepare the Chicken: Start** this by trimming any excess fat from the chicken breasts. Then pat them dry with paper towels to help the seasoning adhere better.

2. **Make the Lemon Herb Marinade:** In a small bowl, combine the fresh lemon juice, lemon zest, minced garlic, chopped rosemary, thyme, parsley, olive oil, honey (if using), salt, and black pepper. Whisk the ingredients together until well combined.

3. **Marinate the Chicken:** To do this, place the chicken breasts in a resealable plastic bag or a shallow dish. Next pour the lemon herb marinade over the chicken, ensuring each piece is well coated. Be sure to seal the bag or cover the dish, and let the chicken marinate in the refrigerator for at least 30 minutes to an hour. For more intense flavor, you can marinate the chicken for up to 8 hours or maybe overnight.

4. **Sear the Chicken (Optional):** For added flavor and color, you can sear the chicken breasts before placing them in the crock pot. To do this, heat a tablespoon of olive oil in a large skillet over medium-high heat. Sear the chicken on both sides until golden brown, about 2-3 minutes per side. This step is optional but enhances the flavor and appearance of the dish.

5. **Place in the Crock Pot:** Transfer the marinated chicken breasts to your mini crock pot (1.5 to 2.5 quarts). Pour the chicken broth over the chicken, ensuring it's partially submerged.

6. **Cook:** Cover the crock pot with its lid and cook on low for 4–6 hours or on high for 2–3 hours, until the chicken is cooked through and reaches an internal temperature of 165°F (74°C).

7. **Rest and Serve:** Once the chicken is cooked, remove it from the crock pot and let it rest on a cutting board for 5 minutes, this allows the juices to redistribute throughout the meat, ensuring it remains tender and juicy.

8. **Garnish and Serve:** Slice the chicken breasts and arrange them on a serving platter. Drizzle with some of the cooking liquid from the crock pot and garnish with additional lemon slices and fresh herbs if desired and serve warm with your choice of sides.

9. **Store and Reheat:** Leftovers can be stored in an airtight container in the refrigerator for up to 3 days. Reheat gently in the microwave or on the stove, adding a splash of chicken broth if needed to keep the chicken moist.

Nutritional Value (Per Serving, Based on 4 Servings)

- **Calories:** Approximately 220 kcal
- **Protein:** 30g
- **Fat:** 9g
- **Carbohydrates:** 4g
- **Fiber:** 1g
- **Sugars:** 1g (from honey)
- **Vitamin C:** 10mg
- **Calcium:** 20mg
- **Iron:** 1mg

Cooking Tips

- **Marinate Longer:** For deeper flavor, marinate the chicken for a few hours or overnight to let the lemon and herbs fully penetrate.

- **Sear for Flavor:** Searing adds a golden crust and enhances the chicken's flavor with a caramelized touch.

- **Balance Acidity:** Adjust lemon juice or add honey if the lemon flavor is too strong. Use Meyer lemons for a milder taste.

- **Use Bone-In Chicken:** Bone-in pieces add flavor and keep the meat tender.

- **Thicken the Sauce:** Simmer the sauce uncovered after cooking or add a cornstarch slurry to thicken.

- **Add Vegetables:** Include baby potatoes, carrots, or green beans to make it a complete meal.

- **Serving Suggestions:** Pair with garlic mashed potatoes, roasted asparagus, or serve over couscous or rice.

Health Benefits

- **High Protein:** Chicken provides lean protein, aiding muscle growth and supporting weight management.

- **Low Fat:** Using skinless breasts keeps it low-fat, while olive oil adds heart-healthy fats.

- **Rich in Antioxidants:** Fresh herbs provide antioxidants that reduce inflammation and protect cells.

- **Immune Support:** Garlic boosts immunity, and lemon juice adds vitamin C for overall health.

- **Aids Digestion:** Lemon juice improves digestion by stimulating enzyme production.

- **Heart Health:** Olive oil and herbs reduce bad cholesterol and inflammation.

- **Bone Health:** Parsley is rich in vitamin K, supporting bone strength and calcium absorption.

- <u>**Hydration:**</u> Lemon juice helps detoxify and balance pH levels.

Lemon Herb Chicken is a flavorful, healthy dish perfect for any meal. Easy to prepare in your mini crock pot, it offers tender, juicy chicken rich in protein, vitamins, and antioxidants. Whether for a weeknight dinner or a special occasion, this recipe is sure to impress and nourish when paired with your favorite sides.

Beef and Sweet Potato Chili

excellent option for a simple, low-effort meal with minimal prep and a lot of flavor.

Preparation Time

- **Prep Time:** 10 minutes
- **Cook Time:** 3-4 hours on low

Serving Size

Servings: 2

Ingredients:

- ½ pound lean ground beef (90% lean or higher)
- One (1) medium sweet potato, peeled and diced
- 1 small onion, diced
- 1 clove garlic, minced
- 1 can (14.5 oz) diced tomatoes
- ½ cup low-sodium beef broth
- 1 tablespoon tomato paste
- 1 teaspoon chili powder
- ½ teaspoon ground cumin
- ½ teaspoon smoked paprika
- ¼ teaspoon ground cinnamon (optional, for sweetness)
- Salt and pepper to taste
- 1 tablespoon olive oil (optional for browning the beef)
- Toppings (optional): Chopped cilantro, shredded cheese, sour cream, avocado

Procedure:

1. **Optional Browning**: Heat 1 tablespoon of olive oil in a skillet over medium heat. Add the ground beef, season with a pinch of salt and pepper,

The Mini Crock Pot Beef and Sweet Potato Chili is a hearty, nutritious meal perfect for dinner. This recipe combines lean ground beef, nutrient-rich sweet potatoes, and a blend of spices to create a flavorful, satisfying dish that's both filling and packed with essential nutrients. It's an

and cook until browned, about 5 minutes. Drain excess fat if necessary. Browning the beef first enhances flavor but can be skipped to save time.

2. **Prepare the Vegetables:** While the beef is browning, peel and dice the sweet potato and chop the onion and garlic.

3. **Combine Ingredients in the Crock Pot:** Add the browned beef (or raw if skipping the browning), diced sweet potato, onion, garlic, diced tomatoes (with their juices), beef broth, tomato paste, chili powder, cumin, smoked paprika, and cinnamon to the mini crock pot. Stir everything to combine.

4. **Cook:** Cover and cook on low for 3-4 hours, or until the sweet potatoes are tender and the flavors have melded together. Stir occasionally to ensure even cooking.

5. **Adjust Seasoning:** Once cooked, taste the chili and adjust seasoning with additional salt, pepper, or spices as needed.

6. **Serve:** Ladle the chili into bowls and top with your choice of garnishes like chopped cilantro, shredded cheese, sour cream, or sliced avocado for extra flavor and texture.

Nutritional Value (Per Serving):

- **Calories:** ~350
- **Protein:** ~25g
- **Fat:** ~15g
- **Carbohydrates:** ~28g
- **Fiber:** ~6g
- **Vitamins & Minerals:** High in vitamin A (from sweet potatoes), iron (from beef), and potassium.

Cooking Tips:

- **Browning the Beef:** While optional, browning the beef before slow cooking adds depth to the flavor. If you're short on time, you can skip this step, but be sure to season the beef well in the crock pot.
- **Sweet Potato Texture:** For a firmer texture, cut the sweet potatoes into larger chunks. If you prefer them to melt into the chili, dice them smaller so they soften more during cooking.
- **Spice Adjustments:** If you like more heat, add crushed red pepper flakes or an extra dash of chili powder. You can also balance the heat with a touch of cinnamon for subtle sweetness.
- **Freezing Leftovers:** This chili stores well in the freezer for up to 3 months. Freeze in individual portions for easy future meals. When reheating, add a splash of broth to thin it out if necessary.

Health Benefits:

- **High in Protein:** The lean ground beef provides a significant amount of high-quality protein, which supports muscle repair, immune function, and overall satiety. Protein also helps the body maintain energy levels throughout the day.

- **Rich in Vitamins and Minerals:** Sweet potatoes are packed with vitamin A, an essential nutrient for eye health and immune function. They also provide a good amount of fiber, which supports digestion and helps keep you full longer.

- **Heart-Healthy Fats:** If you add avocado or use olive oil, you're incorporating heart-healthy fats into the dish. These fats really help reduce inflammation and support the cardiovascular health.

- **Low in Carbohydrates:** This chili is lower in carbs than traditional versions because sweet potatoes are used instead of starchy beans. This makes it a great option for people following low-carb or paleo diets.

- **Anti-Inflammatory Spices:** The chili powder, cumin, and smoked paprika provide antioxidants and anti-inflammatory benefits, supporting overall health and reducing inflammation in the body.

- **Balanced Meal:** With a combination of protein, healthy fats, and fiber-rich carbohydrates, this chili is a well-rounded meal that will keep you full and satisfied without being overly heavy or calorie-dense.

This Mini Crock Pot Beef and Sweet Potato Chili is an easy, nutrient-dense dinner option that's perfect for busy weeknights. With its balance of lean protein, fiber, and heart-healthy fats, it's both delicious and nutritious, making it a go-to meal for anyone looking for a satisfying, wholesome supper.

Chapter 4.

Pasta and Grains

Introduction to Pasta and Grains

In "Pasta and Grains," we delve into the comforting and versatile world of hearty, grain-based dishes. This chapter offers a selection of recipes that showcase the satisfying texture and flavor of pasta, rice, and other grains, all enhanced by the slow cooking process. Whether you're in the mood for a creamy risotto, a layered lasagna, or a simple yet flavorful rice dish, these recipes provide the perfect balance of convenience and indulgence. Designed to be both filling and nutritious, these dishes are ideal for family dinners, meal prepping, or when you simply crave a warm, comforting bowl of goodness.

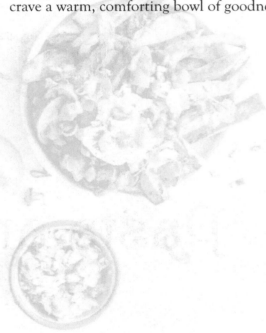

Cheesy Broccoli Rice Casserole

and flavors that everyone will love. This recipe is easy to prepare using your mini crock pot, making it an ideal choice for busy weeknights or casual gatherings. The slow cooking process allows the ingredients to meld together, creating a creamy, cheesy, and irresistibly tasty dish that's sure to become a family favorite.

Preparation Time

- **Prep Time:** 15 minutes
- **Cooking Time:** 2–3 hours on high or 4–6 hours on low
- **Total Time:** 2 hours and 15 minutes to 6 hours and 15 minutes

Ingredients

- Broccoli florets: 3 cups (fresh or frozen, thawed)
- Long-grain white rice: 1 cup (uncooked)
- Chicken broth (low sodium): 2 cups
- Cheddar cheese (shredded): 2 cups
- Cream of mushroom soup (condensed): 1 can (10.5 ounces)
- Onion (finely chopped): 1 small
- Garlic (minced): 3 cloves
- Butter: 2 tablespoons
- Milk: 1 cup (whole or your preferred type)
- Salt: 1 teaspoon (adjust to taste)
- Black pepper: ½ teaspoon (adjust to taste)
- Paprika: ½ teaspoon (optional, for added flavor and color)
- Parmesan cheese (grated): ¼ cup (optional, for topping)
- Breadcrumbs: ½ cup (optional, for a crunchy topping)

Cheesy Broccoli Rice Casserole is a comforting and satisfying dish that combines tender broccoli, fluffy rice, and a rich, cheesy sauce into one delicious casserole. It's the perfect side dish or main course, offering a delightful blend of textures

Serving Size

Serves: 4–6

Procedure

1. **Prepare the Ingredients:** Start by chopping the onion finely and mincing the garlic. If using fresh broccoli, cut it into bite-sized florets. If you're using frozen broccoli, ensure it's thawed and drained of excess water.

2. **Sauté the Onion and Garlic:** In a medium skillet, melt the butter over medium heat. Add the chopped onion and sauté for 5 minutes, until softened and translucent. Then again, add the minced garlic and sauté for another minute, until fragrant.

3. **Combine Ingredients in the Crock Pot:** In your mini crock pot (1.5 to 2.5 quarts), add the uncooked rice, sautéed onion and garlic, chicken broth, milk, cream of mushroom soup, salt, pepper, and paprika (if using). Next, stir to combine all the ingredients well.

4. **Add the Broccoli:** Gently fold in the broccoli florets, ensuring they are evenly distributed throughout the rice mixture.

5. **Cook:** Cover the crock pot with its lid and cook on high for 2–3 hours or on low for 4–6 hours, until the rice is tender and the liquid is absorbed.

6. **Add the Cheese:** About 30 minutes before the cooking time is up, stir in the shredded cheddar cheese. Replace the lid and continue cooking until the cheese is fully melted and the casserole is creamy and thickened.

7. **Optional Topping:** If you prefer a crunchy topping, mix the grated Parmesan cheese with breadcrumbs. Sprinkle this mixture over the top of the casserole during the last 15 minutes of cooking. You can also place the crock pot insert under the broiler for a few minutes to brown the top, but only if your crock pot insert is oven-safe.

8. **Serve:** Once the casserole is done, give it a final stir and taste to adjust the seasoning. Serve the casserole warm, garnished with additional cheese or fresh herbs if desired.

9. **Store and Reheat:** Leftovers can be stored in an airtight container in the refrigerator for up to 3 days. Reheat gently in the microwave or in the oven until warmed through.

Nutritional Value (Per Serving, Based on 6 Servings)

- **Calories:** Approximately 320 kcal
- **Protein:** 12g
- **Fat:** 18g
- **Carbohydrates:** 28g
- **Fiber:** 3g
- **Sugars:** 3g

- <u>Vitamin A:</u> 900 IU
- <u>Vitamin C:</u> 40mg
- <u>Calcium:</u> 250mg
- <u>Iron:</u> 1.5mg

Cooking Tips

- <u>Choose the Right Rice</u>: Long-grain white rice absorbs flavors well. If using brown rice, increase the cooking time.

- <u>Prevent Soggy Broccoli:</u> For crunchier broccoli, add it halfway through cooking.

- <u>Customize Cheese:</u> Mix in cheeses like mozzarella for gooeyness or Gruyère for a nuttier flavor.

- <u>Thicken the Casserole:</u> Let it sit uncovered for 10–15 minutes after cooking, or stir in more cheese.

- <u>Make It Healthier:</u> Use reduced-fat cheese, milk, or homemade cream of mushroom soup with Greek yogurt.

- <u>Add Protein:</u> Fold in cooked chicken, turkey, or ham for a heartier meal.

- <u>Vegetarian Option:</u> Use vegetable broth and add more veggies like mushrooms or spinach.

- <u>High in Calcium:</u> Cheese and milk provide calcium for strong bones and muscle function.

- <u>Good Protein Source:</u> Cheese, milk, and broccoli offer protein for muscle maintenance and satiety.

- <u>Rich in Fiber:</u> Broccoli and rice add fiber for digestive health and cholesterol control.

- <u>Vitamins:</u> Broccoli provides vitamins C, K, and A for immune function, bone health, and vision.

- Heart Health: Healthy fats from olive oil and cheese, plus antioxidants in broccoli, support cardiovascular health.

- <u>Weight Management:</u> Protein, fiber, and healthy fats help keep you full and support weight control.

- <u>Immune Boost:</u> Broccoli's antioxidants and garlic's antibacterial properties strengthen the immune system.

- <u>Bone Health:</u> Calcium, vitamin K, and magnesium support strong bones and prevent osteoporosis.

Health Benefits

Cheesy Broccoli Rice Casserole is a comforting, nutritious dish that's easy to prepare. Combining cheese, broccoli, and rice, it offers a balanced meal or side dish with protein, calcium, and fiber. Perfect for family dinners or potlucks, this casserole is both satisfying and healthful.

Slow Cooker Lasagna

weeknights, family gatherings, or when you simply crave a hearty, home-cooked meal without spending hours in the kitchen.

Preparation Time

- **Prep Time:** 25 minutes
- **Cooking Time:** 4–6 hours on low or 2–3 hours on high
- **Total Time:** 4 hours and 25 minutes to 6 hours and 25 minutes

Ingredients

- Ground beef (or ground turkey): 1 pound
- Onion (diced): 1 medium
- Garlic (minced): 4 cloves
- Olive oil: 1 tablespoon
- Marinara sauce: 3 cups (homemade or store-bought)
- Tomato paste: 2 tablespoons
- Ricotta cheese: 1 ½ cups
- Egg: 1 large
- Fresh parsley (chopped): ¼ cup
- Fresh basil (chopped): ¼ cup (optional)
- Mozzarella cheese (shredded): 2 cups
- Parmesan cheese (grated): ½ cup
- Lasagna noodles (uncooked): 8–10 sheets (regular or no-boil)
- Salt: 1 teaspoon (adjust to taste)
- Black pepper: ½ teaspoon (adjust to taste)
- Red pepper flakes: ¼ teaspoon (optional, for heat)

Serving Size

Serves: 6

Procedure

Slow Cooker Lasagna is a comforting and delicious dish that transforms the classic Italian favorite into an easy, hands-off meal. Layers of tender pasta, rich meat sauce, creamy ricotta, and gooey mozzarella cheese come together beautifully in your slow cooker, making this lasagna incredibly flavorful and satisfying. By using your mini crock pot, you can enjoy all the flavors of traditional lasagna with minimal effort and mess. This recipe is perfect for busy

1. **Prepare the Meat Sauce:** In a large skillet, heat the olive oil over medium heat. Go ahead and add the diced onion and sauté for 5 minutes until softened and translucent. Next, add the minced garlic and cook for another minute until fragrant. Add the ground beef (or turkey) to the skillet, breaking it up with a wooden spoon as it cooks. Cook until the meat is browned and fully cooked through, about 8-10 minutes. Drain any excess fat.

2. **Add Tomato Sauce:** Stir in the marinara sauce, tomato paste, salt, black pepper, and red pepper flakes (if using) into the skillet with the cooked meat. Let the sauce simmer for 5-10 minutes to allow the flavors to meld together. Remove from heat and set aside.

3. **Prepare the Ricotta Mixture:** In a medium bowl, combine the ricotta cheese, egg, chopped parsley, and fresh basil (if using). Mix until well combined. This mixture will add creaminess and flavor to the lasagna layers.

4. **Layer the Lasagna in the Crock Pot:** Lightly grease the inside of your mini crock pot (1.5 to 2.5 quarts) with olive oil or non-stick spray. Begin by spreading a thin layer of the meat sauce on the bottom of the crock pot. Place a layer of lasagna noodles over the sauce, breaking them as needed to fit the shape of the crock pot. Spread a layer of the ricotta mixture over the noodles, followed by a layer of shredded mozzarella and grated Parmesan cheese. Repeat these layers—meat sauce, noodles, ricotta, mozzarella, and Parmesan—until you run out of ingredients or reach the top of the crock pot. Finish with a final layer of meat sauce and a generous sprinkle of mozzarella and Parmesan cheese.

5. **Cook:** Cover the crock pot with its lid and cook on low for 4–6 hours or on high for 2–3 hours. The lasagna is done when the noodles are tender and the cheese is melted and bubbly.

6. **Rest and Serve:** Once the lasagna is cooked, turn off the crock pot and let it sit with the lid on for about 15 minutes. This helps the lasagna set and makes it easier to slice and serve. Use a large spoon or spatula to scoop out portions of the lasagna. Serve hot, garnished with additional fresh parsley or basil if desired.

7. **Store and Reheat:** Leftovers can be stored in an airtight container in the refrigerator for up to 3 days. Reheat individual portions in the microwave or oven until warmed through, this lasagna also freezes well for up to 3 months—simply thaw overnight in the refrigerator before reheating.

Nutritional Value (Per Serving, Based on 6 Servings)

- **Calories:** Approximately 450 kcal
- **Protein:** 28g
- **Fat:** 24g
- **Carbohydrates:** 28g
- **Fiber:** 3g
- **Sugars:** 8g
- **Vitamin A:** 900 IU
- **Vitamin C:** 10mg
- **Calcium:** 400mg
- **Iron:** 3mg

Cooking Tips

- **Use No-Boil Noodles:** Save time with no-boil lasagna noodles; just ensure they're fully covered in sauce to soften.

- **Customize the Meat:** Swap ground beef with turkey, chicken, sausage, or make it vegetarian with mushrooms and spinach.

- **Cheese Options:** Experiment with provolone, fontina, or ricotta salata for added flavor.

- **Layering Tip:** Fully cover each noodle with sauce and cheese to prevent drying out.

- **Thicker Lasagna:** Use fewer, thicker layers for heartier slices.

- **Let It Rest:** Resting after cooking helps the lasagna set for easier slicing and better flavor.

- **Make Ahead:** Assemble up to 24 hours in advance, refrigerate, and cook when ready.

- **Serving Suggestions:** Pair with a green salad, garlic bread, and a glass of red wine for a classic meal.

Health Benefits

- **High Protein:** Provides essential protein from meat and cheese for muscle maintenance.

- **Rich in Calcium:** Cheese and ricotta offer calcium for strong bones and teeth.

- **Vitamins & Minerals:** Tomato sauce adds vitamins A and C, while garlic and onions boost antioxidants.

- **Immune Support:** Garlic's antibacterial properties and onions' antioxidants strengthen the immune system.

- **Energy Boost:** Pasta provides carbs for quick energy, balanced with protein and fats for sustained levels.

- <u>Heart Health:</u> Use lean meats and whole-grain noodles to make it more heart-healthy.

- <u>Bone Health:</u> Rich in calcium and phosphorus, essential for strong bones.

- <u>Comforting:</u> Lasagna is not just nutritious but also comforting, enhancing well-being when shared with loved ones.

Slow Cooker Lasagna is a comforting, easy-to-make dish that's rich in flavor and nutrients. Your mini crock pot simplifies the process, allowing you to enjoy a classic Italian meal with minimal effort. Packed with protein, calcium, and vitamins, this lasagna is both delicious and nourishing.

Mushroom Risotto

Mushroom Risotto is a creamy, luxurious dish that combines the earthy flavors of mushrooms with the rich, velvety texture of arborio rice. Traditionally, risotto requires constant stirring on the stove, but with the help of your slow cooker, you can achieve the same creamy consistency with much less effort. This recipe is perfect for a cozy dinner at home or as an impressive side dish for a special occasion. The slow-cooking process allows the flavors to meld beautifully, resulting in a dish that is both comforting and elegant.

Preparation Time

- **Prep Time:** 20 minutes
- **Cooking Time:** 2–3 hours on high
- **Total Time:** 2 hours and 20 minutes to 3 hours and 20 minutes

Ingredients

- Arborio rice: 1 ½ cups
- Mushrooms (cremini, shiitake, or a mix, sliced): 2 cups
- Onion (finely chopped): 1 small
- Garlic (minced): 3 cloves
- Olive oil: 2 tablespoons
- Butter: 2 tablespoons
- White wine (optional): ½ cup
- Vegetable broth (low sodium): 4 cups (divided)
- Parmesan cheese (grated): ½ cup (plus extra for serving)
- Fresh parsley (chopped): ¼ cup (for garnish)
- Fresh thyme (chopped): 1 tablespoon (optional)
- Salt: 1 teaspoon (adjust to taste)
- Black pepper: ½ teaspoon (adjust to taste)
- Heavy cream: ¼ cup (optional, for extra creaminess)

Serving Size

Serves: 4–6

Procedure

1. **Prepare the Ingredients:** Start by cleaning and slicing the mushrooms,

then finely chop the onion and mince the garlic.

2. <u>**Sauté the Mushrooms:**</u> In a large skillet, heat the olive oil and 1 tablespoon of butter over medium heat. Add the sliced mushrooms and cook for 5-7 minutes, stirring occasionally, until the mushrooms are browned and have released their moisture. Next, remove the mushrooms from the skillet and set aside.

3. <u>**Sauté the Onion and Garlic:**</u> In the same skillet, add the remaining 1 tablespoon of butter. Add your chopped onion and then sauté for 5 minutes until softened and translucent. Add the minced garlic and cook for another minute until fragrant.

4. <u>**Deglaze with White Wine (Optional):**</u> Pour the white wine into the skillet with the onions and garlic, stirring to deglaze the pan and scrape up any browned bits. Cook for 2-3 minutes until the wine has reduced by half. This step adds depth of flavor but can be skipped if you prefer to keep the dish alcohol-free.

5. <u>**Combine in the Slow Cooker:**</u> Transfer the sautéed onions, garlic, and deglazed wine mixture to your slow cooker (1.5 to 2.5 quarts). Add the arborio rice, cooked mushrooms, salt,

black pepper, and fresh thyme (if using). Stir to combine.

6. <u>**Add Broth:**</u> Pour 3 cups of vegetable broth over the rice mixture in the slow cooker. Next, stir gently to make sure the rice is evenly distributed.

7. <u>**Cook:**</u> Cover the slow cooker with its lid and cook on high for 2-3 hours, until the rice is tender and has absorbed most of the liquid. Check the risotto occasionally and add the remaining 1 cup of broth as needed to achieve the desired consistency.

8. <u>**Finish with Cheese and Cream:**</u> Once the rice is cooked and creamy, stir in the grated Parmesan cheese and heavy cream (if using). The Parmesan adds a rich, savory flavor, while the cream enhances the risotto's velvety texture. You should at this point, taste and adjust the seasoning with more salt and pepper if needed.

9. <u>**Serve:**</u> Spoon the risotto into bowls and garnish with chopped fresh parsley and extra grated Parmesan cheese. Serve warm as a main course or a side dish.

10. <u>**Store and Reheat:**</u> Leftovers can be stored in an airtight container in the refrigerator for up to 3 days. Reheat gently on the stove or in the microwave, adding a splash of broth or

water to loosen the risotto if it has thickened.

Nutritional Value (Per Serving, Based on 6 Servings)

- **Calories:** Approximately 350 kcal
- **Protein:** 8g
- **Fat:** 15g
- **Carbohydrates:** 45g
- **Fiber:** 2g
- **Sugars:** 3g
- **Vitamin D:** 8 IU (from mushrooms)
- **Calcium:** 120mg
- **Iron:** 2mg

Cooking Tips

- **Use Arborio Rice:** Arborio rice is key for creamy risotto. Other short-grain options like Carnaroli also work well.

- **Sauté for Flavor:** Sautéing mushrooms, onions, and garlic enhances the risotto's flavor, creating a more complex dish.

- **Check Consistency:** Risotto should be creamy and slightly loose. Check midway and add broth as needed for tender, al dente rice.

- **Enhance Flavor:** Add soy sauce or Worcestershire when sautéing for an umami boost.

- **Vegan Option:** Use plant-based butter, nutritional yeast, and non-dairy milk for a vegan version.

- **Add Veggies:** Include peas, spinach, or asparagus for extra nutrition; add delicate veggies at the end.

- **Pairing:** Serve with a green salad, roasted veggies, or grilled protein, and enjoy with white wine.

Health Benefits

- **Antioxidants:** Mushrooms provide antioxidants like selenium, which boost immunity and reduce inflammation.

- **Vitamin D Source:** Mushrooms offer vitamin D, crucial for bone health and immunity, especially in winter.

- **High in Fiber:** Arborio rice and mushrooms add fiber, aiding digestion and stabilizing blood sugar.

- **Heart Health:** Olive oil offers heart-healthy fats, while garlic and onions support cardiovascular health.

- **Immune Support:** Garlic and onions boost immunity with antibacterial and antiviral properties.

- **Bone Health:** Parmesan adds calcium for strong bones, and cream (if used) provides vitamin K.

- **Low Glycemic Index:** Arborio rice helps maintain stable blood sugar, making it suitable for diabetes management.

- **B Vitamins:** Mushrooms provide B vitamins for energy, brain function, and healthy skin.

Mushroom Risotto is a creamy, flavorful dish that's easy to make in a slow cooker. Rich in nutrients like antioxidants, fiber, and vitamins, it's a healthy, comforting option for any meal. Serve it as a main course or side dish, and enjoy its elegant taste with minimal effort.

Chapter 5

Vegetarian Delights

Introduction to Vegetarian Delights

The "Vegetarian Delights" offers a vibrant collection of plant-based recipes that are both nutritious and flavorful. Whether you're a committed vegetarian or simply looking to incorporate more meatless meals into your diet, this chapter showcases the versatility and richness of vegetarian cuisine. The following recipes celebrate the natural flavors and textures of vegetables, legumes, and grains. Each dish is designed to be wholesome, easy to prepare, and bursting with deliciousness, proving that vegetarian cooking can be just as satisfying and diverse as any other.

Stuffed Bell Peppers

S tuffed Bell Peppers are a vibrant and nutritious dish that brings together a variety of flavors and textures. Each bell pepper is filled with a hearty mixture of rice, beans, vegetables, and spices, creating a delicious and balanced meal that's as pleasing to the eye as it is to the palate. This recipe is incredibly versatile, allowing you to customize the filling to suit your tastes or dietary preferences. Perfect for a family dinner or meal prepping for the week, these stuffed bell peppers are easy to make and packed with nutrients, making them a go-to dish for anyone looking to enjoy a wholesome, satisfying meal.

Preparation Time

- **Prep Time:** 20 minutes
- **Cooking Time:** 4–5 hours on low or 2–3 hours on high
- **Total Time:** 4 hours and 20 minutes to 5 hours and 20 minutes

Ingredients

- Bell peppers (any color): 4 large
- Cooked rice (white, brown, or wild): 1 cup
- Black beans (canned, drained and rinsed): 1 can (15 ounces)
- Onion (finely chopped): 1 small
- Garlic (minced): 3 cloves
- Tomatoes (diced): 1 cup (fresh or canned)
- Corn kernels (fresh or frozen): 1 cup
- Cheddar cheese (shredded): 1 cup (optional, for topping)
- Fresh cilantro (chopped): ¼ cup
- Olive oil: 2 tablespoons
- Ground cumin: 1 teaspoon
- Chili powder: 1 teaspoon
- Dried oregano: 1 teaspoon
- Salt: 1 teaspoon (adjust to taste)
- Black pepper: ½ teaspoon (adjust to taste)
- Lime juice: 1 tablespoon (optional, for added flavor)
- Vegetable broth: 1 cup (for slow cooker)

- Optional Toppings: Sour cream, avocado slices, additional cilantro, or hot sauce

Serving Size

Serves: 4

Procedure

1. <u>Prepare the Bell Peppers:</u> Start by washing the bell peppers thoroughly. Cut off the tops of each pepper and remove the seeds and membranes inside. If the peppers do not stand upright, you can slightly trim the bottom to create a flat base, being careful not to cut through the pepper. Set the prepared peppers aside.

2. <u>Cook the Filling:</u> In a large skillet, heat the olive oil over medium heat. Add the finely chopped onion and sauté for 5 minutes until softened and translucent. Add the minced garlic and cook these for another minute until fragrant.

3. <u>Combine the Filling Ingredients:</u> To the skillet with the onion and garlic, add the cooked rice, black beans, diced tomatoes, corn, ground cumin, chili powder, dried oregano, salt, and black pepper. Stir well to combine and cook for 5-7 minutes until the mixture is heated through and the flavors have melded together. If using, stir in the lime juice and chopped cilantro at the end for a burst of fresh flavor.

4. <u>Stuff the Peppers:</u> Spoon the filling mixture into each of the prepared bell peppers, packing it in gently but firmly. Fill each pepper to the top. If desired, sprinkle a little shredded cheddar cheese on top of the filling in each pepper.

5. <u>Set Up the Slow Cooker:</u> Pour the vegetable broth into the bottom of your slow cooker (1.5 to 2.5 quarts) to create a flavorful steam bath for the peppers. Place the stuffed peppers upright in the slow cooker, ensuring they are snug but not overcrowded.

6. <u>Cook:</u> Cover the slow cooker with its lid and cook on low for 4-5 hours or on high for 2-3 hours, until the peppers are tender but still hold their shape. The filling should be hot and the cheese (if using) should be melted and bubbly.

7. <u>Serve:</u> Carefully remove the stuffed peppers from the slow cooker using tongs. Serve them warm, garnished with additional cilantro, a dollop of sour cream, avocado slices, or a drizzle of hot sauce, if desired.

8. <u>Store and Reheat:</u> Leftovers can be stored in an airtight container in the refrigerator for up to 3 days, reheat in the microwave or oven until warmed through. These stuffed peppers also freeze well for up to 3 months—simply

thaw overnight in the refrigerator before reheating.

Nutritional Value (Per Serving, Based on Four (4) Servings)

- **Calories:** Approximately 300 kcal
- **Protein:** 10g
- **Fat:** 12g
- **Carbohydrates:** 42g
- **Fiber:** 10g
- **Sugars:** 7g
- **Vitamin A:** 3000 IU
- **Vitamin C:** 150mg
- **Calcium:** 150mg
- **Iron:** 3.5mg

Cooking Tips

- **Choose the Right Peppers:** Use large, firm bell peppers that stand upright. Red, yellow, and orange are sweeter, while green offers a traditional flavor.

- **Pre-Cook the Rice:** Ensure the rice is fully cooked before adding it to the filling for the best texture and flavor absorption.

- **Customize the Filling:** Add veggies like zucchini or mushrooms, or switch black beans for kidney beans. For a non-vegetarian option, include ground turkey or beef.

- **Cheese Options:** Mix cheese into the filling or top the peppers with it. For extra spice, be sure to use pepper jack cheese.

- **Prevent Soggy Peppers:** Reduce cooking time or cook on high to keep peppers firm. Also avoid adding too much liquid to your slow cooker here.

- **Make It Vegan:** Omit or use plant-based cheese, and ensure all ingredients are vegan-friendly.

- **Serving Suggestions:** Pair with a salad, garlic bread, or roasted veggies. Add lime juice or salsa for extra flavor.

Health Benefits

- **High in Fiber:** Rice, beans, and veggies provide fiber for digestive health, blood sugar regulation, and satiety.
- **Rich in Vitamins:** Bell peppers offer vitamins A and C, which support immunity, skin health, and vision.

- **Plant-Based Protein:** Black beans provide protein for muscle repair and immune function.

- **Supports Heart Health:** Beans, olive oil, and veggies offer fiber, healthy fats, and antioxidants.

- **Weight Management:** Low in calories but nutrient-dense, helping you feel full and avoid overeating.

- <u>**Low in Saturated Fat:**</u> Naturally low in saturated fat, promoting healthy cholesterol levels.

- <u>**Boosts Immunity:**</u> High in vitamin C and containing garlic and onions, which have antibacterial properties.

- <u>**Balanced Nutrition:**</u> Offers a mix of carbs, protein, and healthy fats for overall well-being.

Stuffed Bell Peppers are nutritious, flavorful, and versatile, perfect for any meal or occasion. High in fiber, vitamins, and plant-based protein, they're healthy without compromising on taste. Easy to customize and visually appealing, they're a must-try for anyone seeking a wholesome, satisfying dish.

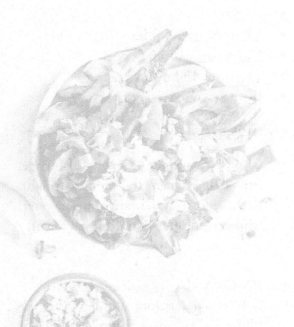

Sweet Potato and Black Bean Chili

wholesome meal for any time of year. The combination of sweet potatoes, beans, and spices creates a deliciously complex dish that is as comforting as it is nutritious. Perfect for a cozy weeknight dinner, meal prepping, or even serving at gatherings, this chili is easy to prepare and brimming with health benefits.

Preparation Time

- **Prep Time:** 15 minutes
- **Cooking Time:** 6–8 hours on low or 3–4 hours on high
- **Total Time:** 6 hours and 15 minutes to 8 hours and 15 minutes

Ingredients

- Sweet potatoes (peeled and diced): 2 large (about 4 cups)
- Black beans (canned, drained, and rinsed): 2 cans (15 ounces each)
- Onion (diced): 1 large
- Garlic (minced): 4 cloves
- Bell pepper (diced): 1 large (any color)
- Tomatoes (canned, diced with juice): 1 can (28 ounces)
- Tomato paste: 2 tablespoons
- Vegetable broth (low sodium): 2 cups
- Chili powder: 2 tablespoons
- Ground cumin: 2 teaspoons
- Smoked paprika: 1 teaspoon
- Ground coriander: 1 teaspoon
- Cayenne pepper: ¼ teaspoon (optional, for heat)
- Salt: 1 teaspoon (adjust to taste)
- Black pepper: ½ teaspoon (adjust to taste)
- Olive oil: 2 tablespoons
- Lime juice: 2 tablespoons (optional, just for serving)

Sweet Potato and Black Bean Chili is a hearty, warming dish that brings together the natural sweetness of sweet potatoes with the earthy richness of black beans, all simmered in a spiced tomato base. This vegetarian chili is packed with flavor and nutrients, making it a satisfying and

- Fresh cilantro (chopped): ¼ cup (optional, for garnish)
- Optional Toppings: Avocado slices, sour cream, shredded cheese, or tortilla chips

Serving Size

Serves: 6

Procedure

1. **Prepare the Vegetables:** Start by peeling and dicing the sweet potatoes into bite-sized cubes. Dice the onion and bell pepper, and mince the garlic.

2. **Sauté the Vegetables (Optional):** In a large skillet, heat the olive oil over medium heat. Add the diced onion and bell pepper, and sauté for 5-7 minutes until softened. Next add the minced garlic and cook for another minute until fragrant. This step helps to enhance the flavor of the chili but can be skipped if you're short on time.

3. **Combine Ingredients in the Slow Cooker:** Transfer the sautéed vegetables (if sautéed) to your slow cooker (3-4 quarts). Add the diced sweet potatoes, drained and rinsed black beans, canned diced tomatoes (with juice), tomato paste, vegetable broth, chili powder, ground cumin, smoked paprika, ground coriander, cayenne pepper (if using), salt, and black pepper. Be sure to stir well to combine all the ingredients.

4. **Cook:** Finally cover the slow cooker with its lid and cook on low for 6-8 hours or on high for 3-4 hours, until the sweet potatoes are tender and the flavors have melded together. At this point, the chili should be thick and hearty.

5. **Finish with Lime and Cilantro:** If using, stir in the lime juice and fresh cilantro just before serving. The lime juice adds a bright, tangy finish that complements the richness of the chili.

6. **Serve:** Ladle the chili into bowls and garnish with your choice of toppings, such as avocado slices, sour cream, shredded cheese, or tortilla chips. Serve hot with cornbread or over rice for a complete meal.

7. **Store and Reheat:** Leftovers can be stored in an airtight container in the refrigerator for up to 4 days, reheat gently on the stove or in the microwave until warmed through. This chili also freezes well for up to 3 months—simply thaw overnight in the refrigerator before reheating.

Nutritional Value (Per Serving, Based on 6 Servings)

- **Calories:** Approximately 320 kcal
- **Protein:** 10g
- **Fat:** 7g
- **Carbohydrates:** 56g
- **Fiber:** 14g

- **Sugars:** 12g
- **Vitamin A:** 18,000 IU
- **Vitamin C:** 50mg
- **Calcium:** 100mg
- **Iron:** 4mg

Cooking Tips

- **Choose Sweet Potatoes:** Pick firm, medium-sized sweet potatoes for the best texture and balance of sweetness.

- **Add Veggies:** Customize with zucchini, corn, or leafy greens like spinach for extra nutrition.

- **Adjust Spice:** Modify the heat by adjusting cayenne or adding chipotle powder, or omit for a milder chili.

- **Thicken the Chili:** Uncover during the last 30 minutes or mash some sweet potatoes to thicken naturally.

- **Make It Smoky:** Add a chipotle pepper in adobo for a smoky, spicy kick.

- **Serving Ideas:** Serve over rice, quinoa, or with cornbread, or top with tortilla chips for crunch.

- **Meal Prep:** Make a large batch; it reheats well and the flavors improve over time.

Health Benefits

- **High Fiber:** Sweet potatoes, beans, and veggies provide fiber for digestion, blood sugar control, and fullness.

- **Rich in Nutrients:** Sweet potatoes offer vitamin A, while peppers and tomatoes provide vitamin C for immunity and skin health.

- **Plant Protein:** Black beans offer protein for muscle repair and satiety.

- **Heart Health:** Fiber, potassium, and antioxidants in this chili support cardiovascular health.

- **Low Fat:** Naturally low in fat, with heart-healthy olive oil.

- **Boosts Immunity:** Garlic, onions, and peppers provide antioxidants that enhance immune function.

- **Blood Sugar Control:** Sweet potatoes help stabilize blood sugar for steady energy.

- **Anti-Inflammatory:** Cumin and paprika reduce inflammation and support overall health.

- <u>**Vegan & Gluten-Free:**</u> Naturally fits a variety of diets, making it versatile and inclusive.

Sweet Potato and Black Bean Chili is a hearty, nutritious dish perfect for any occasion. Packed with fiber, vitamins, and plant-based protein, it's a healthy, flavorful meal that's easy to customize and ideal for meal prep. Whether for dinner or sharing with friends, this chili is sure to become a favorite.

Mediterranean Chickpea Stew

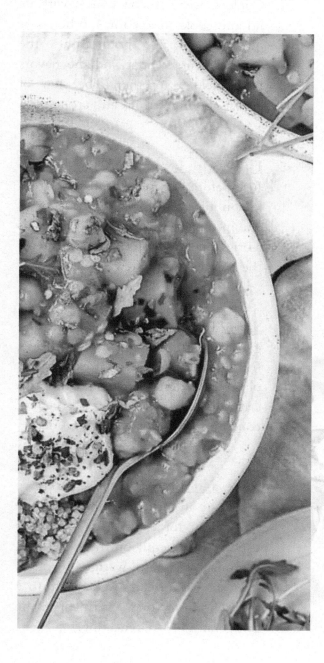

nutritious and satisfying meal that's perfect for any time of year. The slow-cooking process allows the flavors to meld beautifully, creating a comforting and aromatic dish that's both wholesome and delicious. Whether you're looking for a simple weeknight dinner or a dish to impress guests, this Mediterranean Chickpea Stew is sure to be a hit.

Preparation Time

- **Prep Time:** 15 minutes
- **Cooking Time:** 4–6 hours on low or 2–3 hours on high
- **Total Time:** 4 hours and 15 minutes to 6 hours and 15 minutes

Ingredients

- Chickpeas (canned, drained, and rinsed): 2 cans (15 ounces each)
- Onion (diced): 1 large
- Garlic (minced): 4 cloves
- Carrots (peeled and chopped): 2 large
- Red bell pepper (diced): 1 large
- Zucchini (diced): 1 medium
- Tomatoes (canned, diced with juice): 1 can (28 ounces)
- Tomato paste: 2 tablespoons
- Vegetable broth (low sodium): 2 cups
- Kalamata olives (pitted and sliced): ½ cup
- Artichoke hearts (canned, drained and chopped): 1 can (14 ounces)
- Olive oil: 2 tablespoons
- Ground cumin: 1 teaspoon
- Ground coriander: 1 teaspoon
- Smoked paprika: 1 teaspoon
- Dried oregano: 1 teaspoon
- Dried thyme: 1 teaspoon
- Salt: 1 teaspoon (adjust to taste)

Mediterranean Chickpea Stew is a flavorful and hearty dish that brings together the vibrant ingredients of the Mediterranean diet, including chickpeas, tomatoes, olives, and a medley of fresh herbs and spices. This plant-based stew is rich in protein, fiber, and healthy fats, making it a

- Black pepper: ½ teaspoon (adjust to taste)
- Fresh parsley (chopped): ¼ cup (for garnish)
- Fresh lemon juice: 2 tablespoons (optional, for serving)
- Optional Toppings: Crumbled feta cheese, fresh basil, or a drizzle of extra virgin olive oil

Serving Size

Serves: 6

Procedure

1. **Prepare the Vegetables:** Start by dicing the onion, garlic, carrots, red bell pepper, and zucchini. Drain and rinse the chickpeas, and chop the artichoke hearts if they are not already quartered.

2. **Sauté the Onion and Garlic:** In a large skillet, heat the olive oil over medium heat, add the diced onion and sauté for 5 minutes until softened and translucent. Add the minced garlic and cook for another minute until fragrant.

3. **Combine Ingredients in the Slow Cooker:** Transfer the sautéed onion and garlic to your slow cooker (3-4 quarts). Add the chopped carrots, diced bell pepper, zucchini, chickpeas, canned tomatoes (with juice), tomato paste, vegetable broth, Kalamata olives, artichoke hearts, ground cumin, ground coriander, smoked paprika, dried oregano, dried thyme, salt, and black pepper. Don't forget to stir well to combine all the ingredients.

4. **Cook:** Cover the slow cooker with its lid and cook on low for 4-6 hours or on high for 2-3 hours, until the vegetables are tender and the flavors have melded together. The stew of course should be thick and aromatic.

5. **Finish with Lemon Juice and Parsley:** Just before serving, stir in the fresh lemon juice (if using) and garnish with chopped parsley. The lemon juice adds a bright, tangy finish that complements the richness of the stew.

6. **Serve:** Ladle the stew into bowls and garnish with crumbled feta cheese, fresh basil, or a drizzle of extra virgin olive oil if desired. Serve warm with crusty bread, pita, or over a bed of couscous or rice for a complete meal.

7. **Store and Reheat:** Leftovers can be stored in an airtight container in the refrigerator for up to 4 days. And as usual, reheat gently on the stove or in the microwave until warmed through. This stew also freezes well for up to 3 months—simply thaw overnight in the refrigerator before reheating.

Nutritional Value (Per Serving, Based on 6 Servings)

- Calories: Approximately 320 kcal
- Protein: 10g
- Fat: 14g

- Carbohydrates: 40g
- Fiber: 12g
- Sugars: 10g
- Vitamin A: 8000 IU
- Vitamin C: 50mg
- Calcium: 120mg
- Iron: 5mg

Cooking Tips

- **Chickpea Choice:** Canned chickpeas are easy, but for better flavor, soak and cook dried chickpeas beforehand.

- **Add Vegetables:** Customize with seasonal veggies like eggplant, spinach, or potatoes.

- **Adjust Spice:** Increase spice with red pepper flakes or more smoked paprika.

- **Thicken the Stew:** Remove the lid in the last 30 minutes or mash some chickpeas to thicken.

- **Vegan Options:** Use dairy-free toppings like tahini or vegan feta.

- **Serving Ideas:** Pair with crusty bread, couscous, or quinoa, and a fresh green salad.

- **Meal Prep:** Make a large batch for easy meals; flavors improve with time.

Health Benefits

- **High Fiber:** Chickpeas and vegetables offer fiber for digestion, blood sugar control, and satiety.

- **Plant Protein:** Chickpeas provide protein for muscle repair and fullness.

- **Vitamins & Antioxidants:** Veggies offer vitamins A and C, supporting immunity and skin health.

- **Heart-Healthy Fats:** Olive oil and olives provide healthy fats that lower cholesterol and reduce inflammation.

- **Weight Management:** High in fiber and protein, this low-calorie stew keeps you full and aids weight control.

- **Blood Sugar Regulation:** Low glycemic ingredients stabilize blood sugar levels.

- **Immune Boost:** Garlic, onions, and tomatoes enhance immune function.

- **Bone Health:** Chickpeas and veggies provide calcium, magnesium, and vitamin K for strong bones.

Mediterranean Chickpea Stew is a flavorful, nutritious dish that's easy to make and perfect for any occasion. Packed with plant protein, fiber, and healthy fats, it's a balanced meal that's both delicious and nourishing. Ideal for meal prep, this stew offers the essence of Mediterranean cuisine in every comforting bowl.

Chapter 6

Desserts and Sweet Treats

Introduction to Desserts and Sweet Treats

Welcome to the Desserts and Sweet Treats chapter, where indulgence meets simplicity. These recipes are designed to satisfy your sweet tooth while keeping preparation effortless, thanks to the convenience of the mini crock pot. From warm, gooey chocolate lava cakes to creamy coconut rice pudding, each recipe offers comforting flavors with minimal hands-on time. Whether you're hosting a dinner party or treating yourself to a solo dessert, these slow-cooked delights will deliver decadent results without the fuss. Embrace the balance of sweetness and wholesome ingredients for desserts that are as nourishing as they are delicious.

Slow-Cooker Cinnamon Apple Crisp

The Slow-Cooker Cinnamon Apple Crisp is a warm, comforting dessert perfect for fall or any time you crave a sweet treat. Packed with tender, cinnamon-spiced apples and topped with a crunchy oat topping, this dessert is easy to prepare and perfect for small gatherings or weeknight indulgences. It's also a healthier alternative to traditional apple pie, with the benefits of oats and less sugar.

Preparation Time

- **Prep Time:** 10 minutes
- **Cook Time:** 2-3 hours on low

Serving Size

Servings: 2

Ingredients:

For the Filling:

- 2 medium apples, peeled, cored, and sliced (Granny Smith or Honeycrisp work best)
- 1 tablespoon fresh lemon juice
- 1 tablespoon maple syrup or honey
- 1 teaspoon ground cinnamon
- ¼ teaspoon ground nutmeg
- ¼ teaspoon vanilla extract

For the Topping:

- ¼ cup rolled oats
- Two (2) tablespoons almond flour (or whole wheat flour)
- Two (2) tablespoons unsalted butter or coconut oil, melted
- 1 tablespoon brown sugar or coconut sugar
- ¼ teaspoon ground cinnamon
- Pinch of salt
- Optional Toppings: Vanilla ice cream, whipped cream, or chopped nuts

Procedure:

1. **Prepare the Apples:** Peel, core, and slice the apples into thin wedges. Toss them in a bowl with lemon juice, maple syrup, cinnamon, nutmeg, and vanilla extract until the apples are evenly coated.

2. **Layer the Apples in the Slow Cooker:** Grease the inside of the mini crock pot with a little butter or non-stick spray. Add the spiced apple mixture to the crock pot and spread it out evenly.

3. **Make the Topping:** In a small bowl, mix together the rolled oats, almond flour, melted butter, brown sugar, cinnamon, and a pinch of salt until it forms a crumbly texture.

4. **Add the Topping:** Sprinkle the oat mixture evenly over the apples, covering them as much as possible.

5. **Cook:** Cover the slow cooker and cook on low for 2-3 hours, or until the apples are tender and the topping is golden and crisp. For a crunchier topping, remove the lid in the last 30 minutes of cooking to allow some moisture to escape.

6. **Serve:** Once done, spoon the warm apple crisp into bowls and serve with your choice of toppings, such as vanilla ice cream or whipped cream.

Nutritional Value (Per Serving):

- **Calories:** ~250
- **Protein:** ~3g
- **Fat:** ~12g
- **Carbohydrates:** ~38g
- **Fiber:** ~5g
- **Sugars:** ~22g
- **Vitamins & Minerals:** Rich in vitamin C from the apples and healthy fats from the almond flour and butter.

Cooking Tips:

- **Apple Choice:** Using a mix of tart and sweet apples, like Granny Smith and Honeycrisp, will give a more complex flavor to the dessert. If you prefer a sweeter crisp, stick with Honeycrisp or Gala apples.
- **Topping Texture:** For a crunchier topping, you can briefly broil the apple crisp in the oven after it's done cooking. Just transfer it to an oven-safe dish and broil for 1-2 minutes until golden brown.
- **Make It Gluten-Free:** Use gluten-free oats and almond flour for a naturally gluten-free dessert. For a dairy-free version, you can just substitute the butter with coconut oil.
- **Sweetness Adjustments:** Feel free to adjust the sweetness by adding more or less maple syrup or brown sugar based on your taste preferences. You can also use stevia or monk fruit sweeteners for a lower-sugar version.
- **Meal Prep:** The apple crisp can be stored in an airtight container in the fridge for up to 3 days. You can reheat individual servings in the microwave for a quick treat.

Health Benefits:

- **Rich in Fiber:** Apples are high in dietary fiber, especially when you leave the skin on. Fiber helps with digestion, promotes heart health, and helps regulate blood sugar levels.

- **Healthy Fats:** The topping includes almond flour and butter (or coconut oil), providing healthy fats. Almond flour is particularly rich in monounsaturated fats and vitamin E, which support heart health and skin protection.

- **Antioxidants from Cinnamon:** Cinnamon is known for its powerful antioxidants, which help reduce inflammation in the body and stabilize blood sugar levels.

- **Reduced Sugar:** This apple crisp uses maple syrup or honey instead of processed sugar for the filling, providing a natural source of sweetness and fewer added sugars. This makes it a healthier option compared to traditional apple desserts.

- **Balanced Dessert:** The combination of oats, apples, and almond flour offers a balanced dessert that includes carbohydrates, healthy fats, and fiber. This helps keep you satisfied without spiking your blood sugar, making it a healthier alternative to sugary treats.

This Slow-Cooker Cinnamon Apple Crisp is a perfect balance of sweetness, warmth, and crunch. It's a healthier dessert option that's easy to make, using simple ingredients and wholesome alternatives like oats, almond flour, and natural sweeteners. Whether enjoyed with a scoop of ice cream or on its own, it's a comforting treat that's sure to please!

Mini Crock Pot Chocolate Lava Cake

Preparation Time

- **Prep Time:** 10 minutes
- **Cook Time:** 1-2 hours on low

Serving Size

Servings: 2

Ingredients:

- ¼ cup all-purpose flour
- ¼ cup granulated sugar
- 2 tablespoons unsweetened cocoa powder
- ¼ teaspoon baking powder
- Pinch of salt
- 3 tablespoons milk (or plant-based milk)
- 1 tablespoon unsalted butter (or coconut oil), melted
- ¼ teaspoon vanilla extract
- 2 tablespoons semi-sweet chocolate chips
- For the Lava Topping:
- 2 tablespoons brown sugar
- 1 tablespoon unsweetened cocoa powder
- ¼ cup hot water
- Optional Toppings: Whipped cream, vanilla ice cream, or fresh berries

The Mini Crock Pot Chocolate Lava Cake is a rich, indulgent dessert perfect for satisfying your chocolate cravings. This recipe features a warm, gooey center surrounded by a moist cake exterior, all made in a mini crock pot for an easy and hassle-free treat. It's a great dessert for special occasions or when you want to treat yourself to something decadent without much effort.

Procedure:

1. **Prepare the Cake Batter:** In a small bowl, whisk together the flour, granulated sugar, cocoa powder, baking powder, and a pinch of salt. Next you add the milk, melted butter, and vanilla extract. Stir until the batter is smooth and free of lumps.

2. <u>Layer the Chocolate Chips:</u> Grease the inside of the mini crock pot with non-stick spray or a small amount of butter. Pour the cake batter into the crock pot and sprinkle the chocolate chips evenly over the batter.

3. <u>Prepare the Lava</u> Topping: In a separate bowl, mix the brown sugar and cocoa powder. Now you sprinkle this mixture evenly over the top of the batter.

4. <u>Add Hot Water:</u> Slowly pour the hot water over the entire mixture in the crock pot. Do not stir. The water will create the gooey, molten center as the cake bakes.

5. <u>Cook:</u> Cover and cook on low for 1-2 hours, or until the cake is set around the edges but still soft in the center. The cake will look like it's floating on a pool of chocolate sauce, which is exactly what creates the molten lava texture.

6. <u>Serve:</u> Scoop out the cake while it's still warm, being sure to include some of the gooey lava from the bottom. Serve with a dollop of whipped cream, a scoop of vanilla ice cream, or fresh berries.

Nutritional Value (Per Serving):

- <u>Calories:</u> ~350
- <u>Protein:</u> ~5g
- <u>Fat:</u> ~15g
- <u>Carbohydrates:</u> ~50g
- <u>Fiber:</u> ~3g
- <u>Sugar:</u> ~35g
- <u>Vitamins & Minerals:</u> Rich in iron and magnesium from the cocoa powder, with a moderate amount of calcium and potassium from the milk and butter.

Cooking Tips:

- <u>Don't Stir the Topping:</u> After you add the hot water, it's important not to stir. The water will sink to the bottom as it cooks, creating the signature molten lava effect.

- <u>Check for Doneness:</u> Since crock pot temperatures can vary, start checking the cake after 1 hour. The edges should be set, but then the center should still be soft and gooey.

- <u>Add Extra Chocolate:</u> For an even richer treat, add a small piece of dark chocolate or a tablespoon of Nutella to the center of the batter before cooking. This will intensify the molten center.

- <u>Make It Gluten-Free:</u> Use a 1:1 gluten-free flour blend in place of all-purpose flour to make this cake gluten-free.

- **Dairy-Free Option**: Substitute the butter with coconut oil and the milk with almond or coconut milk for a dairy-free version of this lava cake.

Health Benefits:

- **Rich in Antioxidants:** Cocoa powder is packed with antioxidants, particularly flavonoids, which are known to support heart health, reduce inflammation, and improve blood circulation.

- **Boosts Iron and Magnesium:** Chocolate, especially dark or semi-sweet varieties, is a good source of iron and magnesium, both essential for energy production and muscle function.

- **Mood-Enhancing Properties:** Chocolate contains compounds like phenylethylamine (PEA), which is known to trigger the release of endorphins and serotonin, improving mood and promoting relaxation. This makes the lava cake not only a treat for the taste buds but also for emotional well-being.

- **Portion Control:** Portion-controlled desserts like this one allow you to indulge in moderation without overdoing sugar or calories.

- **Dairy-Free and Gluten-Free Adaptable:** By using plant-based ingredients and gluten-free flour, this recipe can easily be adapted for various dietary preferences.

The Mini Crock Pot Chocolate Lava Cake is an indulgent yet easy-to-make dessert that's perfect for any chocolate lover. With its warm, gooey center and rich chocolate flavor, it's a crowd-pleaser that can be prepared with minimal effort. Not only does it satisfy your sweet tooth, but it also offers some nutritional benefits from the cocoa, making it a treat you can enjoy in moderation!

Slow-Cooker Coconut Rice Pudding

coconut, making it a delightful comfort dessert. Perfect for serving warm or cold, this pudding is easy to prepare and perfect for satisfying your sweet tooth with minimal effort.

Preparation Time

- Prep Time: 5 minutes
- Cook Time: 2-3 hours on low

Serving Sizes

Servings: 2

Ingredients:

- ½ cup arborio rice (or any short-grain rice)
- 1 ½ cups full-fat coconut milk (canned)
- ½ cup water
- 3 tablespoons maple syrup (or sweetener of choice)
- ½ teaspoon vanilla extract
- ¼ teaspoon ground cinnamon
- Pinch of salt
- Toppings (optional): Fresh berries, toasted coconut flakes, chopped nuts, or a drizzle of honey

Procedure:

1. **Prepare the Rice:** Rinse the arborio rice under cold water to remove any excess starch. This helps keep the pudding from becoming too sticky.

2. **Combine Ingredients in the Slow Cooker:** In the mini crock pot, combine the rinsed rice, coconut milk, water, maple syrup, vanilla extract, cinnamon, and a pinch of salt. Stir

The Slow-Cooker Coconut Rice Pudding is a rich and creamy dessert made with coconut milk, rice, and a touch of sweetness. This dairy-free version of traditional rice pudding offers a velvety texture and subtle tropical flavor from the

everything together to ensure the rice is evenly coated.

3. <u>Cook:</u> Cover and cook on low for 2-3 hours, stirring occasionally to prevent the rice from sticking to the bottom. The pudding is ready when the rice is tender and the mixture has thickened.

4. <u>Adjust the Consistency:</u> If the pudding becomes too thick as it cooks, stir in a little more coconut milk or water until you reach your desired consistency.

5. <u>Serve:</u> Once the pudding is creamy and cooked through, serve it warm or let it cool. Top with fresh berries, toasted coconut, or chopped nuts for extra texture and flavor.

Nutritional Value (Per Serving):

- <u>Calories:</u> ~350
- <u>Protein:</u> ~4g
- <u>Fat:</u> ~22g
- <u>Carbohydrates:</u> ~36g
- <u>Fiber:</u> ~3g
- <u>Sugars:</u> ~12g
- <u>Vitamins & Minerals</u>: Rich in iron, magnesium, and potassium from the coconut milk and rice.

Cooking Tips:

- <u>Rice Choice:</u> Arborio rice is ideal for this recipe because its high starch content creates a creamy texture. However, you can also use other short-grain rice, such as sushi rice or jasmine rice, for a similar effect. Long-grain rice is not recommended, as it won't yield the same creaminess.

- <u>Stirring:</u> Stir the pudding occasionally during cooking to prevent the rice from sticking and ensure even cooking.

- <u>Adjusting Sweetness:</u> Maple syrup gives this pudding a natural sweetness, but you can adjust the amount to your taste or substitute it with honey, agave syrup, or even coconut sugar for a more tropical flavor.

- <u>Serving Variations:</u> This pudding can be served warm, straight from the slow cooker, or chilled for a cooler, refreshing treat. It thickens as it cools, so you can loosen it up with extra coconut milk if necessary.

- <u>Make It Creamier:</u> If you prefer a richer pudding, replace some of the water with extra coconut milk or even add a splash of plant-based creamer.

- <u>Storage:</u> Store any leftovers in an airtight container in the refrigerator for up to 3 days. Reheat on the stovetop or in the microwave, adding a little coconut milk to loosen it if needed.

Health Benefits:

- **Dairy-Free and Vegan:** Coconut rice pudding is naturally dairy-free and vegan, making it a perfect option for those with lactose intolerance or following a plant-based diet.

- **Rich in Healthy Fats:** Coconut milk is high in medium-chain triglycerides (MCTs), which are fats that are quickly metabolized by the body, providing a quick source of energy. These fats can help support brain function and may improve heart health.

- **Good Source of Iron:** Both coconut milk and rice contain iron, an essential mineral that helps transport oxygen throughout the body. Incorporating foods rich in iron can help prevent fatigue and boost energy levels.

- **Supports Digestive Health:** Rice is gentle on the digestive system and can be particularly soothing for those with sensitive stomachs. The fiber from the rice and coconut milk can also aid in digestion and help regulate bowel movements.

- **Low in Added Sugar:** This recipe uses maple syrup as a natural sweetener, which provides a sweet taste without causing major blood sugar spikes, making it a better option for managing energy levels.

- **Gluten-Free:** Made without wheat or gluten-containing ingredients, this rice pudding is a safe and satisfying dessert option for those with gluten sensitivities or celiac disease.

The Slow-Cooker Coconut Rice Pudding is an easy-to-make, indulgent dessert that's perfect for a cozy night in or a special treat. With its creamy texture, subtle coconut flavor, and health benefits from natural ingredients, this pudding is a deliciously wholesome option that can be enjoyed by everyone. Serve it warm or chilled, with your favorite toppings, for a delightful sweet treat that satisfies your cravings without the guilt!

Bonus Chapter

Instant Pot Magic

Introduction to Instant Pot Magic

Congratulations! As a special thank you for diving into this book, you've unlocked a bonus chapter filled with my top 4 easiest and most mouthwatering Instant Pot recipes. Consider this your reward for embracing the journey of cooking with health and flavor in mind. Whether you're in the mood for melt-in-your-mouth butter chicken, ultra-creamy mac and cheese, or zesty lemon garlic salmon, these recipes are all about making gourmet meals with minimal effort. You've already made a smart choice by picking up this book—now let's take your kitchen skills to the next level with these time-saving, flavor-packed dishes!

Here's to more delicious moments with less stress, just for you!

Instant Pot Butter Chicken

Preparation Time

- **Preparation:** 10 minutes
- **Cooking:** 20 minutes (+10 minutes pressure release)
- **Total Time:** 40 minutes

Ingredients (Serves 4)

- 1 ½ lbs boneless, skinless chicken thighs (cut into bite-sized pieces)
- 2 tbsp butter or ghee
- 1 large onion, chopped
- 3 garlic cloves, minced
- 1 tbsp fresh ginger, grated
- 1 tbsp garam masala
- 1 tsp cumin
- 1 tsp coriander
- 1 tsp smoked paprika
- 1 tsp turmeric
- 1 tsp chili powder (adjust to taste)
- 1 (14.5 oz) can tomato sauce
- ½ cup heavy cream (or coconut cream for dairy-free)
- ½ cup plain Greek yogurt (optional for extra creaminess)
- Salt and pepper, to taste
- ¼ cup fresh cilantro, chopped (for garnish)

Serving Suggestions

- Serves 4 people
- Best served with basmati rice or naan.

Procedure

1. **Sauté Aromatics:** Set the Instant Pot to Sauté. Melt butter and sauté the onion for 2-3 minutes until soft. Add your garlic and ginger, and then cook for another minute until fragrant.

This Instant Pot Butter Chicken is a quick and easy version of the classic Indian dish. Tender chicken pieces are simmered in a rich, creamy tomato-based sauce with fragrant spices. Ready in under 40 minutes, it's perfect for a weeknight meal that tastes like it came from your favorite Indian restaurant!

2. <u>Toast Spices:</u> Add garam masala, cumin, coriander, paprika, turmeric, and chili powder. Stir for about 30 seconds to toast the spices.

3. <u>Add Chicken & Tomato Sauce:</u> Add chicken pieces, stirring to coat in spices. Pour in tomato sauce, season with salt and pepper, and stir well.

4. <u>Pressure Cook:</u> Secure the lid and set the Instant Pot to Manual/Pressure Cook on High for 10 minutes. Now allow a natural pressure release for 10 minutes, then quick release any remaining pressure.

5. <u>Finish with Cream:</u> Open the lid, stir in heavy cream (or coconut cream), and let simmer on Sauté for 2 minutes to thicken. Stir in Greek yogurt if desired.

6. <u>Serve</u>: Garnish with fresh cilantro and serve hot with rice or naan.

Nutritional Information (Per Serving)

- <u>Calories:</u> 390
- <u>Protein:</u> 25g
- <u>Fat:</u> 26g
- <u>Carbohydrates:</u> 12g
- <u>Fiber:</u> 3g
- <u>Sodium:</u> 600mg

Cooking Tips

- <u>Use Chicken Thighs:</u> They stay tender and juicy, making them ideal for pressure cooking.

- <u>Adjust Spice Level:</u> Reduce chili powder for a milder flavor or increase for more heat.

- <u>Dairy-Free Option:</u> Swap heavy cream for coconut cream to make the dish dairy-free without sacrificing the creamy texture.

- <u>Thickening the Sauce:</u> Simmer longer after adding cream if you want a thicker sauce. You can also add a tablespoon of tomato paste during cooking for extra richness.

- <u>Add Yogurt for Extra Creaminess:</u> If you prefer a richer sauce, stirring in Greek yogurt at the end enhances creaminess.

Health Benefits

- <u>High in Protein:</u> Each serving provides 25g of protein, essential for muscle growth and repair.

- <u>Antioxidant-Rich Spices:</u> Spices like turmeric, cumin, and coriander provide antioxidants, with turmeric offering anti-inflammatory benefits.

- <u>Digestive Support:</u> Garlic and ginger help with digestion and may boost immunity.

- <u>Healthy Fats:</u> The butter or ghee provides good fats, while the optional coconut cream offers metabolism-boosting MCTs.

-

- <u>Lower in Carbs:</u> This dish is naturally low in carbohydrates, making it suitable for low-carb or keto diets, especially if served with cauliflower rice instead of traditional rice.

This Instant Pot Butter Chicken is a delicious, healthier take on a beloved classic. It's quick, creamy, and packed with flavor, making it a great option for both busy weeknights and special occasions. Plus, it offers a balance of protein, healthy fats, and antioxidants, giving you both a comforting and nutritious meal!

Instant Pot Beef Stew

stovetop. Perfect for a cozy dinner, it's a one-pot meal that satisfies everyone at the table.

Preparation Time

- **Preparation:** 15 minutes
- **Cooking:** 35 minutes (plus 10 minutes for pressure release)
- **Total Time:** 60 minutes

Ingredients (Serves 6)

- 2 pounds beef stew meat (chuck roast, cut into 1-2 inch cubes)
- 2 tablespoons olive oil
- 1 large onion, chopped
- 3 cloves garlic, minced
- 4 carrots, sliced into thick rounds
- 3 medium potatoes, diced
- 3 stalks celery, chopped
- 2 tablespoons tomato paste
- 4 cups beef broth (low sodium)
- 1 cup red wine (optional, for depth of flavor)
- 2 tablespoons Worcestershire sauce
- 1 teaspoon dried thyme
- 1 teaspoon dried rosemary
- 2 bay leaves
- Salt and pepper, to taste
- 2 tablespoons cornstarch (optional, for thickening)
- Fresh parsley for garnish

Serving Size

- Serves 6 people
- Pair with crusty bread or serve alone for a complete meal.

Procedure

1. **Brown the Beef:** Set your Instant Pot to Sauté mode and heat the olive oil.

This Instant Pot Beef Stew is a hearty, comforting dish packed with tender beef, flavorful vegetables, and a rich broth. With the help of the Instant Pot, you can make a deeply flavorful stew in a fraction of the time it would normally take on the

Season the beef with salt and pepper, then brown the beef in batches, ensuring each side gets a good sear (about 5 minutes per batch). After, remove the browned beef and set aside.

2. <u>Sauté Vegetables:</u> In the same pot, add the chopped onion, garlic, carrots, and celery. Sauté for 2-3 minutes until the onions are translucent and the vegetables begin to soften.

3. <u>Add Tomato Paste and Liquids:</u> Stir in the tomato paste and cook for 1 minute. Then, pour in the red wine, using it to deglaze the pot (scraping up any browned bits stuck to the bottom). Next, add in the beef broth, Worcestershire sauce, thyme, rosemary, and bay leaves. Return the beef to the pot.

4. <u>Add Potatoes and Pressure Cook:</u> Toss in the diced potatoes and give everything a good stir. Secure the Instant Pot lid, set the valve to Sealing, and choose the Manual/Pressure Cook setting on High for 35 minutes. Once cooking is done, allow a natural pressure release for 10 minutes, then carefully do a quick release.

5. <u>Thicken the Stew (Optional):</u> If you prefer a thicker stew, mix 2 tablespoons of cornstarch with 2 tablespoons of cold water, then stir this slurry into the stew. Set the

Instant Pot to Sauté and let it simmer for 2-3 minutes until thickened.

6. <u>Serve:</u> Remove the bay leaves, taste for seasoning, and garnish with fresh parsley. Now serve hot, with crusty bread on the side if desired.

Nutritional Information (Per Serving)

- <u>Calories:</u> 410
- <u>Protein:</u> 32g
- <u>Fat:</u> 18g
- <u>Carbohydrates:</u> 28g
- <u>Fiber:</u> 4g
- <u>Sodium:</u> 650mg

Cooking Tips

- Use chuck roast for tender, flavorful meat that holds up well to pressure cooking.

- Deglaze the pot after browning the meat with wine or broth to lift up flavorful browned bits.
- Thicken the stew with a cornstarch slurry for a heartier consistency, if desired.

- Add red wine for depth, or substitute with more broth if avoiding alcohol.

- Swap vegetables like parsnips or sweet potatoes for variety.

Health Benefits

- **High in protein**: Each serving offers 32g of protein, vital for muscle repair and overall health.

- **Rich in nutrients:** Vegetables add fiber, vitamins A, C, K, and potassium for immune and heart health.

- **Supports joint health:** Beef provides collagen and gelatin, beneficial for bones and joints.

- **Low in sugar:** Ideal for maintaining steady energy levels and managing blood sugar.

- **Satisfying:** The mix of protein, fiber, and broth makes this stew filling and perfect for a balanced meal.

Instant Pot Mac and Cheese

This Instant Pot Mac and Cheese is a quick, creamy, and delicious version of a classic comfort food. Ready in under 15 minutes, it's perfect for weeknights, potlucks, or whenever you need a comforting meal with minimal effort. The Instant Pot makes the process easy—no draining required!

Preparation Time

- **Preparation:** 5 minutes
- **Cooking:** 4 minutes (plus 5 minutes pressure release)
- **Total Time:** 15 minutes

Ingredients (Serves 6)

- 16 oz elbow macaroni (or pasta of choice)
- 4 cups water or low-sodium chicken broth
- 2 tablespoons butter
- 1 teaspoon salt
- 1 teaspoon garlic powder (optional)
- 2 cups shredded sharp cheddar cheese
- 1 cup shredded mozzarella (or another melting cheese like Monterey Jack)
- 1 cup whole milk (or half-and-half for creaminess)
- ½ cup cream cheese (optional, for extra creaminess)
- Ground black pepper, to taste

Serving Size

- Serves 6 people
- Pair with a side salad or veggies for a balanced meal.

Procedure

1. **Add Ingredients to the Instant Pot:** Add the elbow macaroni, water (or broth), butter, salt, and garlic powder (if using) into the Instant Pot. Stir now to combine, ensuring that the pasta is submerged in the liquid.

2. **Pressure Cook:** Secure the Instant Pot lid, set the valve to Sealing, and select the Manual/Pressure Cook setting on High for 4 minutes. Once the cooking time is complete, allow a quick pressure release by carefully turning the valve to Venting.

3. **Add Cheese and Milk:** Once the pressure has been released, open the lid and give the pasta a quick stir. Set the Instant Pot to Sauté mode and gradually stir in the cheddar cheese, mozzarella, and milk until the cheese melts and the sauce becomes creamy. If you're using cream cheese, stir it in as well for extra creaminess.

4. **Serve:** Once the cheese is fully melted and incorporated, turn off the Instant Pot. Be sure to season with freshly ground black pepper and serve immediately.

Nutritional Information (Per Serving)

- **Calories:** 450
- **Protein:** 19g
- **Fat:** 22g
- **Carbohydrates:** 46g
- **Fiber:** 2g
- **Sodium:** 600mg

Cooking Tips

- You can use broth instead of water for that extra flavor.

- Add cream cheese for extra creaminess.

- Mix different cheeses like gouda or gruyere for a richer taste.

- Shred your own cheese for better melting; and yes, avoid pre-shredded cheese.

- Be sure to not overcook the pasta to keep it from becoming mushy.

- Boost nutrition by adding veggies or cooked proteins like chicken or bacon.

Health Benefits

- **Rich in calcium:** The cheese and milk provide essential calcium for bone health.

- **High in protein:** Each serving offers 19g of protein, making it satisfying and filling.

- **Easily customizable:** Adding vegetables like peas or broccoli increases fiber and vitamins.

- **Energy-boosting:** The carbs in the pasta provide quick energy.

- **Healthy fats:** Whole milk and butter provide fats that support brain and hormone health.

- **Lower sodium option:** Use low-sodium broth and adjust salt levels for a heart-healthier dish.

Instant Pot Mac and Cheese is the perfect blend of creamy, cheesy comfort and convenience. It's easy to make, endlessly customizable, and provides a good balance of nutrients when paired with vegetables or lean proteins. With just 15 minutes of cooking time, you can enjoy a homemade, satisfying meal that will please the whole family!

Instant Pot Lemon Garlic Salmon

salmon, keeping it tender and moist while infusing it with bright lemon and garlic flavors. It's a light, refreshing dish that pairs well with veggies, quinoa, or a side of rice for a nutritious meal.

Preparation Time

- **Preparation:** 5 minutes
- **Cooking:** 7 minutes (plus time for pressure release)
- **Total Time:** 15 minutes

Ingredients (Serves 4)

- 4 (6 oz) salmon fillets (skin on or off)
- 2 tablespoons olive oil
- 3 cloves garlic, minced
- 1 lemon, sliced thinly
- ½ cup water
- 2 tablespoons lemon juice
- 1 teaspoon dried or fresh thyme
- Salt and pepper, to taste
- Fresh parsley, for garnish

Serving Size

- Serves 4 people
- Serve with steamed vegetables, quinoa, or a side of rice.

Procedure

1. **Prepare the Salmon:** Season the salmon fillets with salt, pepper, and thyme. Drizzle olive oil over the fillets and rub the minced garlic evenly on top. Place a thin slice of lemon on each fillet for extra flavor.

2. **Prepare the Instant Pot:** Pour ½ cup of water and 2 tablespoons of lemon

This Instant Pot Lemon Garlic Salmon is a quick, flavorful, and healthy meal that comes together in under 15 minutes. The Instant Pot perfectly steams the

juice into the Instant Pot. Place the trivet inside the pot to elevate the salmon above the liquid. This ensures the salmon steams perfectly rather than boiling in water.

3. **Add the Salmon:** Place the salmon fillets on the trivet, making sure they're not overlapping. If your Instant Pot is small, cook in batches.

4. **Pressure Cook:** Secure the lid, set the valve to Sealing, and select the Manual/Pressure Cook setting on High for 3 minutes. Once the cooking time is complete, allow a natural pressure release for 5 minutes, then perform a quick release for any remaining pressure.

5. **Serve:** Open the lid carefully and transfer the salmon to plates. Garnish with fresh parsley and an additional squeeze of lemon juice, if desired. Serve this immediately with your favorite side dishes.

Nutritional Information (Per Serving)

- **Calories:** 280
- **Protein:** 25g
- **Fat:** 18g
- **Carbohydrates:** 2g
- **Fiber:** 0g
- **Sodium:** 320mg

Cooking Tips

- **Use the Trivet:** Always place the salmon on the trivet to ensure it steams rather than boils. This keeps the texture of the salmon firm and tender.

- **Fresh or Frozen Salmon:** You can use frozen salmon fillets for this recipe, but increase the cooking time by 1 minute. Make sure they're separated before cooking.

- **Adjust Cooking Time:** If your salmon fillets are thicker than 1 inch, increase the pressure cooking time by 1 minute to ensure they cook through.

- **Don't Overcook:** You should be careful not to overcook the salmon. It should flake easily with a fork when done but remain moist inside.

- **Add Flavor Variations:** Feel free to experiment with other herbs like dill or rosemary, or add a sprinkle of red pepper flakes for a hint of heat.

- **Meal Prep Friendly:** You can easily double the recipe and store leftovers in the fridge for up to 3 days. Reheat gently to avoid overcooking.

Health Benefits

1. **Rich in Omega-3 Fatty Acids:** Salmon is one of the best sources of omega-3 fatty acids, which are essential for

heart health, reducing inflammation, and supporting brain function.

2. <u>High in Protein:</u> With 25g of protein per serving, this salmon dish provides plenty of high-quality protein that supports muscle repair, boosts metabolism, and keeps you feeling full longer.

3. <u>Supports Brain Health:</u> The omega-3 fatty acids found in salmon are also crucial for brain health. They can improve cognitive function and may help protect against age-related mental decline.

4. <u>Low in Carbs:</u> This meal is naturally low in carbohydrates, making it an excellent choice for those on low-carb or keto diets.

- <u>Loaded with Antioxidants</u>: Garlic and lemon not only add flavor but are also

rich in antioxidants, which protect the body from oxidative stress.

- <u>Promotes Heart Health:</u> The olive oil used in this recipe contains monounsaturated fats, which are known to lower bad cholesterol (LDL) levels and increase good cholesterol (HDL), promoting overall cardiovascular health.

- <u>Low in Calories:</u> At only 280 calories per serving, this dish is light yet filling, making it a great option for those looking to maintain or lose weight while still getting essential nutrients.

With heart-healthy fats, high-quality protein, and a quick cook time, this recipe makes healthy eating both delicious and convenient. Pair it with a variety of sides to create a balanced, wholesome meal the whole family will love.

Your 28-day Meal Plan

Here's a 28-day meal plan using the recipes from you, designed to offer variety while staying balanced and nourishing. Each day includes breakfast, lunch (featuring a soup or stew), and dinner. Desserts are added periodically to offer a treat.

Week 1

Day 1

Breakfast	Cinnamon Apple Oatmeal (Chapter 1)
Lunch	Hearty Chicken Noodle Soup (Chapter 2)
Dinner	Pulled BBQ Chicken (Chapter 3)

Day 2

Breakfast	Overnight Vanilla Almond Quinoa (Chapter 1)
Lunch	Creamy Tomato Basil Soup (Chapter 2)
Dinner	Garlic Herb Pork Tenderloin (Chapter 3)

Day 3

Breakfast	Veggie-Packed Breakfast Casserole (Chapter 1)
Lunch	Beef and Barley Stew (Chapter 2)
Dinner	Lemon Herb Chicken (Chapter 3)

Day 4

Breakfast	Mini Crock Pot Southwest Egg Scramble (Chapter 1)
Lunch	Creamy Lentil and Spinach Soup (Chapter 2)
Dinner	Slow Cooker Lasagna (Chapter 4)

Day 5

Breakfast	Cinnamon Apple Oatmeal (Chapter 1)
Lunch	Hearty Chicken and Vegetable Stew (Chapter 2)
Dinner	Three-Bean Chili (Chapter 3)

Day 6

Breakfast	Slow-Cooker Banana Nut Quinoa Porridge (Chapter 1)
Lunch	Creamy Tomato Basil Soup (Chapter 2)
Dinner	Dinner: Mushroom Risotto (Chapter 4)

Day 7

Breakfast	Veggie-Packed Breakfast Casserole (Chapter 1)
Lunch	Beef and Barley Stew (Chapter 2)
Dinner	Stuffed Bell Peppers (Chapter 5)
Dessert	Slow-Cooker Cinnamon Apple Crisp (Chapter 6)

Week 2

Day 8

Breakfast	Mini Crock Pot Southwest Egg Scramble (Chapter 1)
Lunch	Hearty Chicken Noodle Soup (Chapter 2)
Dinner	Beef and Sweet Potato Chili (Chapter 3)

Day 9

Breakfast	Overnight Vanilla Almond Quinoa (Chapter 1)
Lunch	Creamy Lentil and Spinach Soup (Chapter 2)
Dinner	Herb Pork Tenderloin (Chapter 3)

Day 10

Breakfast	Cinnamon Apple Oatmeal (Chapter 1)
Lunch	Hearty Chicken and Vegetable Stew (Chapter 2)
Dinner	Mediterranean Chickpea Stew (Chapter 5)

Day 11

Breakfast	Slow-Cooker Banana Nut Quinoa Porridge (Chapter 1)
Lunch	Beef and Barley Stew (Chapter 2)
Dinner	Cheesy Broccoli Rice Casserole (Chapter 4)

Day 12

Breakfast	Veggie-Packed Breakfast Casserole (Chapter 1)
Lunch	Creamy Tomato Basil Soup (Chapter 2)
Dinner	Pulled BBQ Chicken (Chapter 3)

Day 13

Breakfast	Mini Crock Pot Southwest Egg Scramble (Chapter 1)
Lunch	Creamy Lentil and Spinach Soup (Chapter 2)
Dinner	Lemon Herb Chicken (Chapter 3)
Dessert	Mini Crock Pot Chocolate Lava Cake (Chapter 6)

Day 14

Breakfast	Overnight Vanilla Almond Quinoa (Chapter 1)
Lunch	Hearty Chicken Noodle Soup (Chapter 2)
Dinner	Sweet Potato and Black Bean Chili (Chapter 5)

Week 3

Day 15

Breakfast	Cinnamon Apple Oatmeal (Chapter 1)
Lunch	Creamy Tomato Basil Soup (Chapter 2)
Dinner	Slow Cooker Lasagna (Chapter 4)

Day 16

Breakfast	Veggie-Packed Breakfast Casserole (Chapter 1)
Lunch	Hearty Chicken and Vegetable Stew (Chapter 2
Dinner	Three-Bean Chili (Chapter 3)

Day 17

Breakfast	Mini Crock Pot Southwest Egg Scramble (Chapter 1)
Lunch	Beef and Barley Stew (Chapter 2)
Dinner	Garlic Herb Pork Tenderloin (Chapter 3)

Day 18

Breakfast	Overnight Vanilla Almond Quinoa (Chapter 1)
Lunch	Creamy Lentil and Spinach Soup (Chapter 2)
Dinner	Stuffed Bell Peppers (Chapter 5)

Day 19

Breakfast	Slow-Cooker Banana Nut Quinoa Porridge (Chapter 1)
Lunch	Hearty Chicken Noodle Soup (Chapter 2)
Dinner	Mushroom Risotto (Chapter 4)

Day 20

Breakfast	Veggie-Packed Breakfast Casserole (Chapter 1)
Lunch	Creamy Tomato Basil Soup (Chapter 2)
Dinner	Beef and Sweet Potato Chili (Chapter 3)
Dessert	Slow-Cooker Coconut Rice Pudding (Chapter 6)

Day 21

Breakfast	Cinnamon Apple Oatmeal (Chapter 1)
Lunch	Hearty Chicken and Vegetable Stew (Chapter 2)
Dinner	Mediterranean Chickpea Stew (Chapter 5)

Week 4

Day 22

Breakfast	Mini Crock Pot Southwest Egg Scramble (Chapter 1)
Lunch	Beef and Barley Stew (Chapter 2)
Dinner	Pulled BBQ Chicken (Chapter 3)

Day 23

Breakfast	Overnight Vanilla Almond Quinoa (Chapter 1)
Lunch	Creamy Lentil and Spinach Soup (Chapter 2)
Dinner	Lemon Herb Chicken (Chapter 3)

Day 24

Breakfast	Slow-Cooker Banana Nut Quinoa Porridge (Chapter 1)
Lunch	Creamy Tomato Basil Soup (Chapter 2)
Dinner	Slow Cooker Lasagna (Chapter 4)

Day 25

Breakfast	Cinnamon Apple Oatmeal (Chapter 1)
Lunch	Hearty Chicken Noodle Soup (Chapter 2)
Dinner	Cheesy Broccoli Rice Casserole (Chapter 4)

Day 26

Breakfast	Veggie-Packed Breakfast Casserole (Chapter 1)
Lunch	Hearty Chicken and Vegetable Stew (Chapter 2)
Dinner	Sweet Potato and Black Bean Chili (Chapter 5)

Day 27

Breakfast	Mini Crock Pot Southwest Egg Scramble (Chapter 1)
Lunch	Beef and Barley Stew (Chapter 2)
Dinner	Three-Bean Chili (Chapter 3)

Day 28

Breakfast	Overnight Vanilla Almond Quinoa (Chapter 1)
Lunch	Creamy Tomato Basil Soup (Chapter 2)
Dinner	Stuffed Bell Peppers (Chapter 5)
Dessert	Slow-Cooker Cinnamon Apple Crisp (Chapter 6)

This plan provides a healthy balance of proteins, vegetables, and grains with lots of variety, along with delicious desserts to enjoy occasionally!

Conclusion

As we conclude this culinary journey, it's time to reflect on the many ways you've learned to harness the power and versatility of the mini Crock-Pot. From breakfast delights to comforting classics, each recipe in this book has showcased the unique advantages of slow cooking. The mini Crock-Pot, often underestimated due to its size, is a powerhouse in the kitchen. It allows you to create deeply flavorful dishes with minimal effort, making it perfect for both novice cooks and seasoned chefs looking for convenience without compromising taste.

You've explored a wide array of recipes, each tailored to maximize the potential of your mini Crock-Pot. Whether you've been preparing hearty soups and stews, experimenting with international flavors, or indulging in decadent desserts, you've likely discovered that slow cooking offers a unique opportunity to develop flavors over time, transforming simple ingredients into extraordinary meals. The mini Crock-Pot is not just a kitchen appliance; it's a tool that encourages mindfulness in cooking, allowing you to take a step back and let the slow, steady heat do the work.

As you master these recipes, you're not only gaining proficiency with your mini Crock-Pot but also deepening your understanding of how ingredients interact over time. You've learned how the gentle, consistent heat of the slow cooker can bring out the natural sweetness of vegetables, tenderize even the toughest cuts of meat, and meld spices into a harmonious blend that's impossible to achieve with quicker cooking methods.

Your Next Steps

Now that you've built a strong foundation, it's time to take your slow cooking skills to the next level. The mini Crock-Pot, while perfect for the recipes in this book, is also an ideal tool for experimentation. Don't be afraid to modify the recipes you've mastered. Add a new spice to your favorite soup, swap out ingredients based on what's in season, or even try cooking dishes that traditionally wouldn't be associated with slow cooking.

One of the greatest joys of mastering a technique is the freedom it gives you to experiment. With slow cooking, you can explore different cuisines, experiment with new ingredients, and even develop your own recipes. For instance, try incorporating different grains, such as quinoa or farro, into your soups and stews. Experiment with plant-based proteins like lentils or chickpeas, or even challenge yourself by creating a slow-cooked dessert that isn't in this book.

Additionally, consider how you can incorporate slow cooking into your weekly meal planning. Use your mini Crock-Pot to prepare make-ahead meals, which can be a lifesaver during busy weeks. Double a recipe and freeze half for a future meal, or prepare overnight oats and stews that can cook while you sleep, making breakfast and dinner hassle-free.

As you expand your culinary skills, don't hesitate to explore new resources. Join online cooking communities, take part in slow cooking challenges, or even share your creations on social media. The slow cooking community is vast and supportive, full of individuals who, like you, appreciate the art of creating flavorful dishes with time and patience.

Final Thoughts

The journey you've embarked on with your mini Crock-Pot is just the beginning. Slow cooking is not just a method; it's a lifestyle choice that emphasizes the importance of time, patience, and enjoying the process. In today's fast-paced world, where quick meals and instant gratification often take precedence, slow cooking offers a refreshing counterbalance. It reminds us to savor the process as much as the result, to appreciate the aromas that fill our kitchens, and to anticipate the pleasure of a well-cooked meal.

As you continue on this journey, remember that the joy of slow cooking lies in its simplicity and its ability to bring people together. Whether you're cooking for yourself, your family, or a gathering of friends, the meals you prepare in your mini Crock-Pot are more than just food—they are expressions of care, comfort, and creativity.

Take pride in the dishes you create, and don't be afraid to revisit the recipes in this book, tweaking and perfecting them as you go. With each use, your mini Crock-Pot becomes more than just an appliance; it becomes a trusted companion in your kitchen adventures, helping you create meals that nourish both body and soul.

In closing, I encourage you to embrace the art of slow cooking fully. Enjoy the journey of discovering new flavors, mastering new techniques, and sharing your culinary creations with those around you. Slow cooking is a timeless skill, one that connects us to the traditions of the past while allowing us to innovate for the future. As you continue to explore, experiment, and enjoy, you'll find that the possibilities with your mini Crock-Pot are truly endless.

Happy cooking, and may your mini Crock-Pot bring you many delicious meals and joyful moments in the kitchen!

<u>Congratulations!</u>

You did it! You've made it to the end and I couldn't be more thrilled to celebrate with you. By now, you've mastered the art of slow cooking, whipping up delicious, fuss-free meals that fit seamlessly into your lifestyle. I hope you've enjoyed every recipe and discovered some new favorites along the way!

Your support and trust in this cookbook mean the world to me, and I would love to hear about your experience. If you found this book helpful, inspiring, or even just fun to cook with, I kindly ask you to leave an honest review on Amazon. Your feedback not only helps others discover the book, but it also helps me continue to create resources that make your kitchen life even easier.

Thank you for being part of this journey. I can't wait to see what you cook up next!